DOW 3000

Thomas Blamer
and
Richard Shulman

Wyndham Books ‖ New York

Published by Wyndham Books
A Simon & Schuster Division of
Gulf & Western Corporation
Simon & Schuster Building
Rockefeller Center
1230 Avenue of the Americas
New York, New York 10020
WYNDHAM and colophon are trademarks
of Simon & Schuster

Designed by Irving Perkins Assoc.

Manufactured in the United States of
America

10 9 8 7 6 5 4 3 2 1

Library of Congress Cataloging in
Publication Data

Blamer, Thomas, date.
  Dow 3000.

    1. Stocks—Prices—United States.
  2. Investments—United States.
  3. Corporations—United States—
  Finance.
  I. Shulman, Richard.   II. Title.   III. Title:
  Dow three thousand.
  HG4915.B56   332.63′22′0973   81-23115
  ISBN 0-671-43224-9   AACR2

DEDICATED TO: My mother, Laurel Blamer, and my grandmother, Marie Nelson, who invested a great deal of love and affection in me.

T.N.B.

My mother, Sally Shulman, and my grandfather, David Kaplow, with gratitude and love.

R.H.S.

ACKNOWLEDGMENTS

WE WOULD LIKE to thank the following individuals who were kind enough to review the manuscript of this book and who offered many helpful suggestions as to how it might be improved: Bruce and Judy Barnett, Bob Gerlicher, Carol Greenly, Bob and Barbara Guberud, Forrest Mars, Tom and Gloria Mayer, Rollie and LeAnn Sullivan, and last but not least, Damon Sedita.

We would also like to thank the Wilson Library of the University of Minnesota, the Ramsey County Library, the James J. Hill Library, and the Minneapolis Public Library for making their facilities available to us.

CONTENTS

The General Forecast

PART I

CHAPTER 1
THE HANDWRITING ON THE WALL

A DOW JONES INDUSTRIAL AVERAGE of 3,000 by December 1989.

You must be kidding!

That would be the response of most investors as this book is being written. Yet ten years ago if a book had been written titled *Gold $800* or *Oil—$35 per Barrel,* it would have been greeted by a similar response. The test of an investment concept is not the skepticism it generates, but rather the logic underlying it.

Most investors failed to take full advantage of the enormous price rises in oil and gold in the last decade. Many of these investors are still upset over this failure. Yet they should not be so harsh with themselves. Anticipating $800 gold and $35 oil in 1980 from the viewpoint of 1970 required extraordinary foresight. One had to foresee the rise of OPEC, the Arab-Israeli War, the fall of the Shah, the seizure of the hostages, the Iran-Iraq War, and a host of economic mistakes by the United States government.

The forecast of a Dow Jones Industrial Average of 3,000 by the end of 1989 does not require such extraordinary foresight. It does not require the occurrence of a number of essentially unpredictable international events. It does not even require that the United States solve its current economic problems. The forces that will bring about a Dow of 3,000 by 1989 are already in effect. The purpose of this book is to acquaint investors with these forces.

Unlike the recent case of gold or oil, those investors who will be kicking themselves in 1989 for having missed the enormous rise in the American stock market in the Eighties will have no

11

excuse. They will have only themselves to blame for having ignored, in the early 1980s, the unmistakable handwriting on the wall.

We make these statements with full awareness that, as we write them, the stock market is plunging, interest rates are rising, and a business recession is looming on the horizon.

The logic calling for a Dow Jones Industrial Average of 3,000 by 1989 is not particularly complicated, although it does involve a few numbers. The basic concept is that common stocks are currently selling far below their underlying value. If they sell for anything near their true value in 1989, the Dow will be at 3,000 or above.

Actually, a forecast of 3,000 on the Dow should not be so startling. Part of the shock results from the magnitude of the numbers used in the Dow Average. Three thousand is a large number, particularly in relation to individual stock prices, which typically range from $10 to $100 per share. If the forecast is phrased in an equivalent way—that the average price of the stocks composing the Dow Jones Industrial Average will rise from under $40 to more than $120—it does not sound so implausible. Essentially what is being forecast is that stock prices will more than triple in this decade. Before you dismiss this prediction out of hand, remember that *stock prices have more than tripled in a decade twice before in this century—in the 1920s and in the 1950s*. In the Twenties the Dow rose from a low of 63.9 to a high of 381.2—an increase of 5.97 times. In the Fifties the Dow rose from a low of 196.8 to a high of 679.4—an increase of 3.45 times. Great fortunes were made in those decades by investors who were able to anticipate those dramatic stock market rises.

Our forecast of Dow 3,000 is derived from two distinct valuation formulas—the Asset Formula and the Earnings Formula. The Asset Formula is based on the idea that a common share is a piece of paper representing part ownership of a real business. If the assets of the business are sold and the corporation is liquidated, the piece of paper entitles its owner to his proportional share of the net proceeds generated. The specific formula employed is Value = Assets – Liabilities. The formula quantifies the concept that ultimately the value of a corporate share is determined by the net assets that it represents.

The Earnings Formula is based on the idea that a common share should be valued by the amount of money that it produces for its owner each year. Specifically, the formula is Value = Earnings × Valuation Factor. This multiple-of-profits approach is widely used in real estate as well as in the stock market. In real estate, the gross income of a building is frequently multiplied by a suitable valuation factor to determine the worth of the building.

The fascinating thing about these two separate valuation approaches is that they both indicate a Dow in excess of 3,000 by 1989. In subsequent chapters, we will explore these valuation approaches in greater detail. We will also discuss the R-Factor, Statement No. 33, and the capital gains tax. These influences have a very great effect on stock market values, but they are not widely understood.

In Part II of this book, we will examine each one of the thirty Dow stocks individually and forecast its 1989 stock price. The rise in some of these individual Dow stocks could be quite spectacular. They could far exceed the rise in the Dow Average itself. We project that certain of them may increase by almost 500 percent. This would be in line with what certain Dow stocks did in the 1950s, the last time the Dow Average tripled in a decade.

Most investors have forgotten how rewarding a true bull market can be. Table I is a list of the current thirty Dow stocks together with the percentage price change they actually experienced in the decade of the 1950s. A 500 percent increase is the equivalent of a stock's going from $50 to $300 per share.

Table II shows how several of the major mutual funds performed during the Fifties. The data reveals the spectacular behavior of actual stock portfolios during this period.

In the 1950s as well as the 1920s, the Dow did not go up continuously. In both decades, the Dow's advance was interrupted by sharp declines. In the period 1920–1921, for example, the Dow dropped 42 percent before beginning its meteoric rise. It is quite possible that as you are reading this book, the Dow will be experiencing or will have recently experienced a substantial drop in price. We would not view such a decline with alarm. Unless it is caused by a change in one of the fundamental mechanisms generating long-term stock prices, such a decline will simply offer another opportunity to buy stocks at very favorable prices. One of the nice things about the stock market is that it frequently

TABLE I

Percentage Price Change, Dec. 1949–Dec. 1959, Rounded to Nearest 50% (Dividends Not Included)

COMPANY	PERCENT
Allied Corporation	+ 150
Alcoa	+ 750
American Brands	+ 50
American Can	+ 50
American Telephone	+ 50
Bethlehem Steel	+ 600
Du Pont	+ 350
Eastman Kodak	+ 550
Exxon	+ 350
General Electric	+ 600
General Foods	+ 350
General Motors	+ 350
Goodyear	+1400
Inco	+ 300
IBM	+ 850
International Harvester	+ 50
International Paper	+ 550
Johns-Manville	+ 100
Merck	+ 450
Minnesota Mining & Mfg.	+1300
Owens-Illinois	+ 200
Procter & Gamble	+ 200
Sears	+ 250
Standard Oil (Cal)	+ 250
Texaco	+ 500
Union Carbide	+ 250
U.S. Steel	+ 650
United Technologies	+ 200
Westinghouse	+ 250
Woolworth	+ 50

TABLE II

Results of $10,000 Investment, Jan. 1, 1950–
Dec. 31, 1959, All Distributions Reinvested

Dreyfus Fund	$55,286
Fidelity Fund	43,651
IDS Stock Fund	42,959
Keystone S-4	77,534
Mass. Investors Growth	54,290
Mass. Investors Trust	47,479
Pioneer Fund	42,039
T. Rowe Price Growth	58,380
United Accum. Fund	47,876

Source: *Investment Companies*, 1960, Arthur Wiesenberger & Co.

offers investors a second and third chance to get aboard a great bull market.

However, before exploring these ideas, let's first examine a crucial question: What happens to all that money?

KEY POINTS

1. ‖ Two separate valuation formulas project a Dow Jones Industrial Average of 3,000 by December 1989.
2. ‖ Stock prices have more than tripled in a decade twice already in this century—the 1920s and the 1950s.
3. ‖ Certain individual stocks in the Dow Jones Industrial Average may increase almost 500 percent by 1989. A 500 percent rise is the equivalent of a $50 stock increasing to $300.
4. ‖ Great bull markets usually offer investors a second or third chance to buy stocks at favorable prices.

CHAPTER 2
WHAT HAPPENS TO ALL THAT MONEY: THE R-FACTOR

MANY YEARS AGO, Mark Twain was on a lecture tour through the United States. At each town on his tour, he was usually introduced to the audience by a distinguished member of the community. In one town, he was introduced by the town's leading lawyer. The lawyer, after a few introductory remarks, made the following statement:

"Ladies and gentlemen, this evening we have with us a person who is extremely rare in America these days. We have with us a humorist who is truly funny. May I present to you Mark Twain."

During all of his remarks, the lawyer had been nervous and had kept his hands in his pockets. At this point, Mark Twain took the podium and said:

"Thank you, Mr. Chairman, for those kind remarks. I must observe, however, that this evening we have with us something that is even rarer in America today than a humorist who is really funny. . . . We have with us a lawyer who keeps his hands in his own pockets."

Corporations today, like the lawyers of Mark Twain's time, have difficulty keeping their hands in their own pockets. In effect, they have their hands in the pockets of their shareholders. There is nothing sinister, however, in this fact. It is actually to the shareholders' benefit, as we shall see.

After paying all expenses, all salaries, and all taxes and after making allowance for the wearing out of plant and equipment,

American corporations had $164.1 billion left over in 1980. In other words, they made profits of this amount. What did they do with this money? Where did it go?

$57.7 billion is easy to trace. This money was sent to the shareholders in the form of dividend checks.

What about the rest of the money? Where did it go? The simple answer is that it didn't go anywhere. It remained in the corporations. The money was used by the corporations for the expansion of their businesses. New plants were built and new assets were acquired. In effect, the corporations held out on their shareholders. This fact has very great implications, yet few investors grasp it. What it means is that the underlying value of corporations is continually increasing. It's as simple as that.

To reiterate: Corporations don't pay out to their shareholders all of the money they make. They hold back a substantial portion of their profits to expand their businesses. Since this money remains in the corporations, it is only common sense that the underlying value of the corporations should increase by the amount of profits held back.

The easiest way to illustrate this principle is to consider a hypothetical savings account which pays 10 percent interest a year tax-free. What would happen to the value of the account if, each year, only one half of the interest were withdrawn? Let's trace what happens in the account for a few years.

If we start with an initial deposit of $1,000, at the end of the first year we will have earned $100 in interest. If we take half of this interest and spend it, we now have $1,050 in the account at the start of year two. During this year we earn $105 in interest. If we take half of this interest ($52.50) and spend it, we have $1102.50 in the account at the start of year three. Following is a table showing the behavior of the account over seven years:

TABLE III

Savings Account at 10%, Half of Interest
Withdrawn Each Year (Figures Rounded)

Year	Beginning Balance	Interest Earned	Interest Withdrawn	Ending Balance
1	$1,000	$100	$50	$1,050
2	1,050	105	53	1,103
3	1,103	110	55	1,158
4	1,158	116	58	1,216
5	1,216	122	61	1,277
6	1,277	128	64	1,341
7	1,341	134	67	1,407

Graphically, the process looks like this:

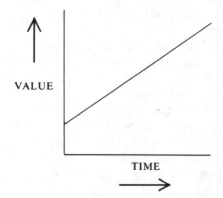

The account is clearly growing in value. Notice how the column marked "Ending Balance" in Table III increases inexorably each year. It would continue to grow indefinitely. There is no magical reason why it increases. It grows simply because each year half of the interest is left in the account. It has to grow under these circumstances. This same process occurs when corporations hold back part of their profits. The only difference is that the reinvested money is going into tangible assets such as land, buildings, and equipment rather than into a savings account.

Lest you think we are fantasizing about companies' holding

back part of their profits, let's take a real-world example. Procter & Gamble is one of America's premier companies. It is considered by many observers to be one of the most astutely managed firms in the country. In 1980, Procter & Gamble earned $643 million selling Crest, Tide, Crisco, Pampers, Folger's Coffee, Charmin, and a host of other products. This money was pure profit. All taxes had been paid. All advertising costs had been paid. All wages and salaries had been paid. An allowance had been made for the wearing out of its plant and equipment. Out of this profit, $281 million was sent to Procter & Gamble shareholders in the form of dividend checks. What happened to the remaining $362 million? Where did it go?

As you have probably guessed, this money stayed in the Procter & Gamble Company. It was used for new facilities to enable Procter & Gamble to continue to expand and to provide new and improved products.

From the standpoint of common sense, it seems quite clear that the value of the Procter & Gamble Company increased by $362 million in 1980. This was the amount of profit that the company held back from its shareholders. If this money had been burned in a fire or dropped from an airplane, one could not say with any conviction that the value of the company had increased. But since the money was in fact used to purchase real assets such as land, buildings, and machinery, the conclusion is inescapable that the value of the company increased.

Procter & Gamble is no different from other corporations when it comes to holding back profits. Almost every major American company retains a sizable part of each year's profits. It should be emphasized that companies retain profits with the best interests of the shareholders in mind. Shareholders must pay income tax at regular rates on dividends. By retaining profits, companies hope to increase the price of their stock so that their shareholders will be able to sell at a profit. If the shareholder has held his stock for more than one year, his profit is taxed at a much lower rate than are dividends.

We call the practice of retaining profits the R-Factor. This factor is the fundamental engine that drives the underlying value of American corporations relentlessly upward. It also furnishes the explanation for the long-term trend of stock prices in the United States.

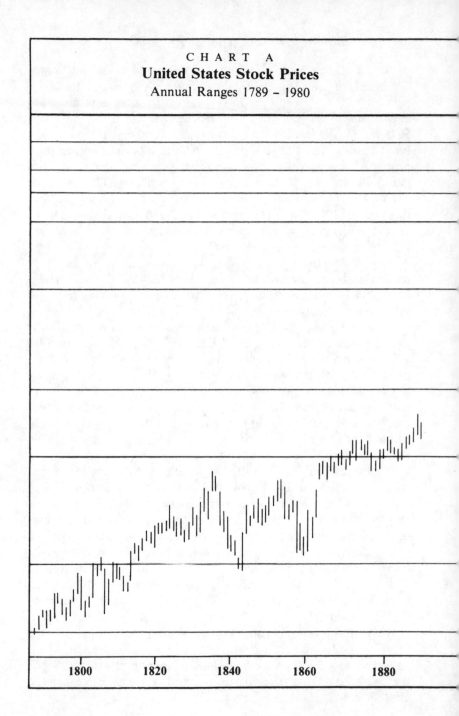

CHART A
United States Stock Prices
Annual Ranges 1789 – 1980

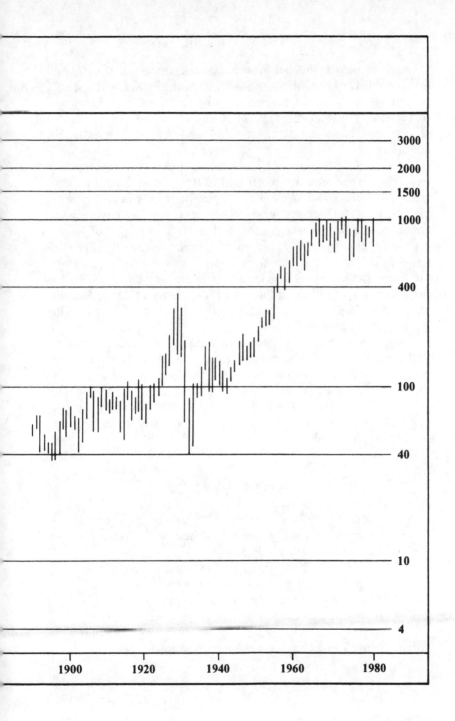

Chart A shows the behavior of stock prices in the United States from 1789 to 1980. It is drawn on a ratio scale so that equal percentage changes are represented by equal vertical distances. Economists consider this type of scale to be most representative of long-term historical data. Very low and very high numbers do not distort it.

The one clear feature of Chart A is that common stock prices have risen over time in the United States. There have been periods of decline and there have been periods when prices remained level for several years, but these periods have always ended with prices moving to a higher level. In light of the R-Factor (retained profit), this behavior is not surprising. Price ultimately reflects value. American corporations have been retaining a substantial part of their profits each year since 1789. It is this retention of profit that has steadily increased their underlying value. And this increased value has been reflected in the rising trend of stock prices.

Chart A very clearly reflects the wisdom of the adage "Don't Sell America Short." A person who sells short is betting that prices will decline. Historically, over the long run, this has been the way to commit financial suicide in the American stock market. The R-Factor (retained profit) implies that this will be as true in the future as in the past. It will thus be wise in the future to remember the adage.

KEY POINTS

1. ‖Corporations retain a sizable part of their profit each year for reinvestment in their businesses. We call this process the R-Factor.
2. ‖The R-Factor (retained profit) causes the underlying value of corporations to grow each year.
3. ‖The R-Factor (retained profit) explains why stock prices in the United States have been in a rising trend for nearly two hundred years and why this trend should reassert itself in the future.

CHAPTER 3

STATEMENT NO. 33

A N EXECUTIVE WAS in the hospital for a heart-transplant operation. On the morning of the operation, the heart surgeon came into the executive's room and told him that there had been an automobile accident the night before in which three men had been killed and that the executive could pick which of the three hearts he wanted transplanted into his body. One of the men killed in the auto accident was a twenty-five-year-old professional athlete. Another was a forty-five-year-old corporate executive. The third was a seventy-year-old banker. Without hesitation, the executive requested that the heart of the seventy-year-old banker be transplanted into his body.

The surgery went off without a hitch, and in a few days the executive found he had more vim and vigor than he had ever had before in his life. On a routine checkup two years later, the heart surgeon found that the executive was still in excellent health. Curious, the doctor asked the executive why he had picked the heart of the seventy-year-old banker instead of that of the twenty-five-year-old professional athlete.

The executive replied: "That's easy. I picked the heart of the seventy-year-old banker because I figured it had never been used."

One of the reasons bankers have earned a reputation for not using their hearts is their requirement that a borrower must demonstrate that there is a very high probability that a loan will be paid back. It is frequently said that the only way to get a loan from a bank is to prove you don't need it.

The way you prove to a banker that you don't really need a

loan is by showing that you have a substantial net worth. To do this, you would take a piece of paper and you would list on it the value of everything you own (your assets). This would include your home, your car, your savings accounts, etc. From the total of these items, you would subtract everything you owe (your liabilities). This would include the mortgage on the house, the car loan, credit card balances, and so forth. The result would be what you are worth financially (your so-called net worth).

On the application for the loan, the banker would probably record the information in the following manner:

Assets		Liabilities	
Home	$100,000	Mortgage on	
Car	5,000	home	$50,000
Bank accounts	10,000	Car loan	2,000
Furnishings	15,000	Credit cards	1,000
Boat	3,000		
Total assets	$133,000	Total liabilities	$53,000
		Net worth	$80,000

When information is recorded in this manner, it is called a balance sheet. The term "balance sheet" comes from the fact that the total of everything on the left side of the page is always equal to the total of everything on the right side of the page. The two sides balance.

Individuals are not the only ones who prepare balance sheets. Bankers require them of corporations also. In addition, publicly held corporations are required by the Securities and Exchange Commission to send their shareholders a report each year which includes a balance sheet of the company.

Procter & Gamble's balance sheet, as of June 30, 1980, looks like this in summary:

Assets		Liabilities	
Total assets	$6.5 billion	Total liabilities	$2.9 billion
		Book Value*	$3.6 billion

* For the sake of clarity in our presentation, we have called this entry "Book Value." On its official balance sheet as published in its annual report, Procter &

It follows the customary practice of listing assets on the left and liabilities on the right. Book Value is the difference between assets and liabilities and is listed on the right side of the balance sheet beneath liabilities. It is the same thing as net worth.

As you might suspect, the key number in this balance sheet is the figure for Book Value. This is what Procter & Gamble shareholders would receive if the company was liquidated, assuming the assets were sold for the amount they are listed at in the balance sheet and assuming that all the debts could be paid off for the amount listed under liabilities. In a liquidation or bankruptcy, all of the assets of the company are sold. The proceeds are used to satisfy the company's liabilities. Any remaining money is distributed to the owners of the company—the shareholders. The shareholders come last. They get what is left over. This can be an advantage or a disadvantage, depending on the size of the liabilities relative to the size of assets. In the case of Procter & Gamble, there is a very comfortable margin.

The term "Book Value" comes from the fact that it is the value of the company as computed from the account books. Book Value (Total Assets − Liabilities) is a rough measure of the liquidating value of a company. It can be very helpful in assessing the worth of a company. A company should be worth at least what it can be liquidated for. This is just common sense. If the assets of a company can be sold for $6 billion and all of the liabilities of the company total $2 billion, the company is clearly worth $4 billion.

The problem with using Book Value (Total Assets − Liabilities) is that it may not accurately reflect the amount that would be left over for the shareholders in the event of bankruptcy or liquidation. This is particularly true today. One major problem is the way assets are valued on the balance sheet.

Book Value today, in most cases, greatly understates the liquidating value of companies. This is because the accounting profession requires that assets be recorded on the balance sheet at their historical cost. For example, a piece of land purchased fifty years ago for $1 million would still be listed on the balance

---

Gamble titles this entry "Shareholders' Equity." As we are using the term, Book Value is equivalent to Shareholders' Equity.

sheet at $1 million today, even though the land could easily be sold for $20 million cash.

In an era of stable prices, historical cost is a reasonable measure of value. It is at least as good as any other measure, and it has the great advantage of being simple to determine. But in an age of inflation, the principle of valuing assets at their historical cost leads to great distortion. Where, for example, can you buy something today at 1965 prices? Yet many assets are carried on corporate balance sheets at 1965 prices.

The inaccuracy of balance sheets based on historical cost has been recognized for several years. However, it has taken the financial community until just recently to adopt measures to rectify the situation. Large companies are now forced to disclose the effects of inflation by Statement of Financial Accounting Standards No. 33, otherwise known as Statement No. 33.

Statement No. 33 requires companies to disclose certain data in the notes to their annual financial reports. In particular, it requires large companies to disclose what is, in effect, an inflation-adjusted Book Value. In this figure, assets are valued at the companies' estimate of their current cost. This inflation-adjusted Book Value is, in most cases, a much more realistic measure of liquidating value than historical cost. It is not based on outdated figures.

These inflation-adjusted Book Values disclose some eye-opening facts about the underlying values of American corporations. For example, Procter & Gamble, on its 1980 balance sheet, reported a Book Value of $3.6 billion. After adjusting for inflation, Procter and Gamble estimates that this figure should be $5.8 billion. That's an increase of 61 percent. Other companies have even more startling revelations contained in their Statement No. 33 data. There can be no doubt that inflation has dramatically driven up the value of corporate assets.

KEY POINTS

1. ‖ The Book Value of a corporation is computed by taking its total assets and then subtracting the cor-

poration's liabilities. Book Value = Total Assets
− Liabilities.

2.‖ Book Value is a rough measure of the liquidating
value of a corporation. Traditionally, it is computed
by valuing assets at their historical cost.

3.‖ The inflation-adjusted Book Value of most corporations, as revealed by their Statement No. 33 data,
is dramatically higher than that based on historical
cost.

CHAPTER 4
THE DOW JONES INDUSTRIAL AVERAGE

THE DOW JONES INDUSTRIAL AVERAGE exerts a great deal of influence over the general esteem in which stockbrokers are held. When the Dow has been strong for several years, brokers are generally held in good repute if their customers have done well. When the Dow declines for a prolonged period, the reverse is true. It is at these times that the most interesting stories are told about stockbrokers.

After a particularly devastating decline, this story circulated. It seems that a stockbroker died of a heart attack on the same day that an elderly bishop died, and they both reached Heaven at the same time. The angel at the gate, after examining their credentials, bid that they both enter. The angel escorted them down a pleasant moss-covered lane until they reached a modest one-room bungalow. At this point, the angel turned to the bishop and said:

"Bishop, this is where you will be spending the rest of eternity."

The bishop smiled and walked alone down the path to the bungalow. The angel and the stockbroker continued along the path until they reached a gigantic mansion. The mansion had formal gardens, a huge swimming pool, seventy-two rooms, and a complete staff. The angel pointed to the mansion and said to the stockbroker:

"Stockbroker, this is where you will be spending the rest of eternity."

The stockbroker turned to the angel and said:

"There must be some mistake. This must be for the bishop, and the one-room bungalow must be mine."

The angel replied:

"There has been no mistake. You see, we have lots of bishops here . . . but you are the first stockbroker."

Despite its name, the Dow Jones Industrial Average was not devised by a man named Dow Jones. It was, in fact, first compiled by a financial journalist, Charles Henry Dow, for use in his publication, *The Wall Street Journal*. Dow's partner in the publishing business was Edward D. Jones, and it was the name of the partnership, Dow Jones, that was extended to the new index.

Actually, Dow and Jones had a third partner in their publishing business, Charles M. Bergstresser. Fortunately for newscasters, Mr. Bergstresser agreed that his name would be too unwieldy to include in the title of the firm. Otherwise, newscasters today might be announcing that the "Dow Jones Bergstresser Industrial Average was up ten points today in active trading."

The Dow Jones Industrial Average was first published in 1896. It was computed with great simplicity. The closing prices of twelve leading industrial stocks were added up, and the resulting total was divided by 12. The twelve stocks used in the first average were:

American Cotton Oil
American Sugar
American Tobacco
Chicago Gas
Distilling and Cattle Feeding
General Electric
Laclede Gas
National Lead
North American
Tennessee Coal and Iron
United States Leather preferred
United States Rubber

Over the years, there have been many changes in the companies in the average. As the composition of the American economy changed, companies were replaced by other, more representative ones. In addition, the average was expanded first to twenty stocks and then to the present thirty. Throughout all of these changes, Dow Jones and Company has attempted to maintain the price continuity of the average. It has done this by means of changing the divisor. Thus today the average is not computed by adding up the price of the thirty stocks and dividing by 30. Instead, the prices are added up and divided by 1.314, as of September 8, 1981. It is this changing of the divisor that allows the current level of the average to be compared directly to the levels of prior years, in spite of substitutions, splits, etc.

Changing the divisor, however, has a disadvantage. It removes the level of the average from the range of actual stock prices. Typically, stock prices run from $10 to $100 per share, whereas the Dow is many times these numbers. When a person unfamiliar with this phenomenon hears that the Dow was up 36 points for the day, it is easy for him to conclude that there has been a dramatic rise. After all, a 36-point rise in a stock selling at 50 or 100 is a huge percentage gain in one day. But a 36-point gain in the Dow when it is at 900, while it would be considered a significant move, only amounts to a 4 percent increase. This is the equivalent of a $50 stock increasing by 2 points.

Table IV shows exactly how the Dow Jones Industrial Average was computed for September 8, 1981. Notice that the closing prices of the thirty stocks were added up and divided by 1.314. Remember, the divisor is at this level to maintain the continuity of the average with prior years.

Interestingly enough, Dow Jones and Company does not actually do the computations involved in determining the price of its own Dow Jones Industrial Average each day. The actual computations are done by an Associated Press computer and then communicated back to Dow Jones so that it may flash the average over its private news service.

If we perform a slightly different computation on the data in Table IV, it is possible to compute what the price of the average stock in the Dow is. If we divide the sum of the closing prices by 30, we arrive at 37.28. Mentally, it seems easier to accept the forecast that this price of the average share will triple in the coming decade than it is to accept the forecast that the Dow Jones Industrial Average itself will go from 1,000 to 3,000. Yet, mathematically, the two propositions are identical. Large numbers tend to play tricks on the mind. It should be noted that in

TABLE IV

Computation of Closing Dow Jones
Industrial Average, Sept. 8, 1981

COMPANY	CLOSING PRICE
Allied Corp.	44.50
Alcoa	25.875
American Brands	38.00
American Can	32.125
American Telephone	54.375
Bethlehem Steel	21.875
Du Pont	39.00
Eastman Kodak	64.50
Exxon	31.50
✓ General Electric	55.00
General Foods	28.00
General Motors	46.125
Goodyear	18.125
INCO	16.25
IBM	54.00
International Harvester	8.50
International Paper	42.375
Johns-Manville	15.625
Merck	82.00
✓ Minnesota Mining & Mfg.	48.875
Owens-Illinois	26.25
✓ Procter & Gamble	68.25
Sears	16.50
Standard Oil (Cal)	39.375
Texaco	35.25
Union Carbide	48.50
U.S. Steel	28.75
United Technologies	42.875
✓ Westinghouse	26.50
Woolworth	19.50
Total	1,118.375
Divisor	1.314

Closing
price   1,118.375/1.314 = 851.12

Price of the
average share 1,118.375/30 = 37.28

Japan, a stock index expressed in large numbers has not prevented the spectacular performance of that market. In 1970, the Nikkei Dow Jones average was at 2,252. By 1981, it was at 7,706. What matters is not how the index is computed, but rather how the underlying stocks perform.

There is no question that the Dow Jones Industrial Average has flaws as a market indicator. It uses only thirty stocks to represent the movement of several thousand listed issues. Statisticians can demonstrate that the way in which the divisor is used distorts its results. At times its performance deviates from the rest of the market. But in spite of these flaws, the Dow is the most widely quoted measure of the stock market. It has the longest history, and it is the simplest to understand. For these reasons, we have chosen the Dow as our focus. In the next few chapters, we will relate the effects of the R-Factor and inflation to the real world of the stock market using the Dow Jones Industrial Average.

Incidentally, for those sharp-eyed readers who are wondering how Chart A, which looks like the Dow Jones Industrial Average from 1789 to 1980, can exist, when the Dow was not computed until 1896, a word of explanation. In compiling Chart A, several historical stock indexes were spliced to the Dow Jones Industrial Average. Thus, Chart A represents the actual performance of the Dow from 1896 and historical stock indexes prior to that. The actual data come from the Foundation for the Study of Cycles Inc., 124 South Highland Avenue, Pittsburgh, PA 15206. Anyone interested in the raw data can obtain it directly from the foundation for a small fee.

KEY POINTS

1.‖ The Dow Jones Industrial Average is computed by adding up the closing prices of the common stocks of thirty leading industrial companies and then dividing by a divisor (currently 1.314).

2.‖ A 36-point move in the Dow Jones Industrial Average when it is at 900 is the equivalent of a $50 stock moving 2 points.

CHAPTER 5
DOW 3000

A FEW YEARS ago, a management consultant from New York was working on a special project at a company headquartered in Miami, Florida. His project required close interaction with the company's top executives, and he observed that they were involved in a bitter dispute with the firm's outside accountants. The executives wanted to reflect some information in the company's financial statements in a certain way, but the accountants refused to allow it. The dispute was so bitter that on several occasions, meetings between the executives and the accountants almost ended in fisticuffs. In the end, the accountants won out, as they refused to certify the statement if their wishes weren't followed.

A few weeks later, the consultant was driving along one of the waterways at the edge of the Everglades when he saw a boat out on the water with two water skiers behind it. As the boat came closer, he saw that two of the company's executives were in the boat, while two of the outside accountants were on water skis behind. He thought to himself that it was nice that the executives and the accountants had been able to patch up their bitter differences and that they were now socializing together.

The boat came close enough to shore so that the consultant was able to yell to the executives:

"Glad to see you fellows are taking the accountants water skiing. It's a good idea to let bygones be bygones."

As the boat passed by, the executives yelled back:

"Water skiing? Heck, we're not water skiing . . . we're trolling for alligators!"

. . .

The moral of the story is that things are not always what they seem. Gilbert and Sullivan said it more poetically: "Things are seldom what they seem. Skim milk masquerades as cream." The same principle, slightly reversed, applies to the Dow Jones Industrial Average at the present time. In the stock market, cream is masquerading as skim milk. Stock values are substantially above current market prices.

The distinction between price and value needs to be clearly drawn. In the long run, price tends to reflect value in the stock market. However, over the shorter term (which can be several years), there can be a substantial gap between price and value. At times price can be driven dramatically above value, as in 1929. At other times price can be driven dramatically below value, as in the Depression. It is the goal of the investor to be able to determine which situation prevails and to act accordingly. This frequently requires substantial patience, but great fortunes have been made by investors who have mastered this skill.

At the present time, the Dow is selling for substantially less than its value. This situation has occurred because the value of the Dow has been rising for the last fifteen years, while its price has remained level. The Dow Jones Industrial Average's closing price was 969 in 1965. It was 964 in 1980. Graphically, this situation can be sketched as follows:

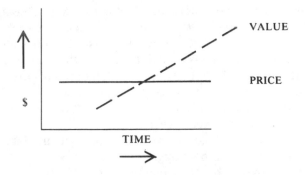

The forces that have caused value to increase are the ones we have been discussing—the R-Factor (retained profits) and inflation. In every year since the Great Depression, the Dow companies, in aggregate, have been profitable. They have made money regardless of wars, price controls, high interest rates, recessions, and taxes. Part of these profits has been paid out as dividends to the shareholders, and part has been retained in the business. The part that has been retained (the R-Factor) has been used to purchase new assets. These new assets have caused the Book Value of the Dow to increase year after year. We can see this very clearly from Chart B.

Chart B is a chart of the Dow Jones Industrial Average and its Book Value during the period 1920–1980. The Book Value shown is the traditional one based on historical cost, unadjusted for inflation. Remember, Book Value is computed by taking total assets and subtracting total liabilities. Total Assets − Liabilities = Book Value.

The chart very clearly shows the effect of the R-Factor (retained profits). Notice how the Book Value line rises steadily. This is as we would expect. New assets purchased with retained profits cause the asset figure on the balance sheet to increase while having no effect on liabilities. The result is an increase in Book Value. Referring to our formula: Total Assets (increasing) − Liabilities (no effect) = Book Value (increasing). That is how the R-Factor influences Book Value. *Retained profits cause Book Value to increase.* There are other factors that can influence it in any particular year, but over time the dominant factor is retained profit.

In any one year, the effect of the R-Factor on Book Value has usually been small—30 or so points in terms of the Dow Jones Industrial Average. That is why it is so easily overlooked. But over time, these additions add up and have a dramatic effect. Since 1965, the R-Factor has added over 450 points to the Book Value of the Dow.

It is also quite apparent from Chart B that stock prices in the long run have reflected Book Value. There has been a very massive increase in Book Value since 1920, and this has been reflected, until recently, by an equally massive rise in the stock market. This phenomenon should not be surprising. Stocks should sell for at least what companies can be liquidated for.

Notice on Chart B how the Dow dropped below Book Value only in 1931–33, 1942, 1949, 1974–75, and 1977–80. We have marked these periods with arrows on the chart. All of these times

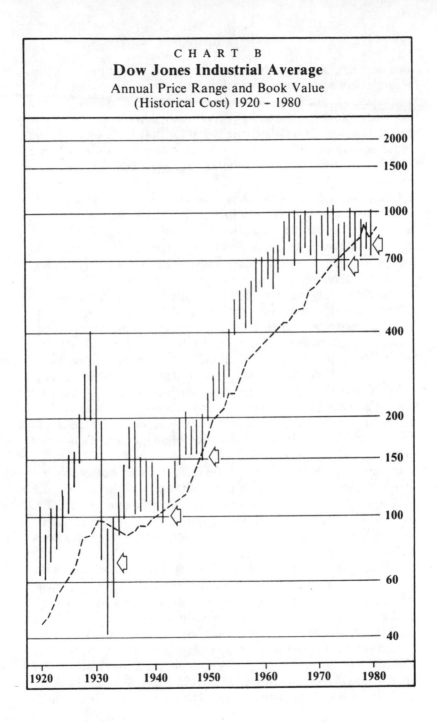

CHART B
Dow Jones Industrial Average
Annual Price Range and Book Value
(Historical Cost) 1920 – 1980

have proved to be exceptionally good times to buy stocks. During these periods, stocks were selling at levels below their Book Value. They were selling for less than the companies could be liquidated for.

So far, we have been looking only at the effect of the R-Factor (retained profit) on Book Value. Now let's add the effect of inflation in order to get a more realistic measure of current liquidating value. Remember, inflation in the last few years has caused a huge increase in the value of corporate assets. Traditional Book Value, as shown in Chart B, does not reflect this tremendous increase because assets are valued at historical cost.

Chart C is the same as Chart B except that the Book Value figures have been adjusted for inflation. They reflect the great effect that inflation has had on asset values. The 1980 figure is based on the data supplied by the Dow companies pursuant to Statement No. 33. Numbers for earlier years are our estimates.

In 1980, the inflation-adjusted Book Value (liquidating value) of the Dow was 1,575. This compares to a closing 1980 price of 964. In other words, price was almost 40 percent below value. Currently the Dow is near 850. Can there be any doubt that the Dow is on the bargain table at the present time?

The startling fact that appears from Chart C is that the Dow, at the end of 1980, was nearly as low as it was in 1932 in the depths of the Depression. Notice how far the 1980 closing price of 964 is below the inflation-adjusted Book Value line. And 1932 was the lowest year in history for this relationship. Investors who purchased stock in 1932 reaped enormous profits over the long run.

The clear message of Chart C is that the Dow, at current price levels, is exceptionally undervalued. It is far below liquidating value. The other conclusion that can be drawn from Chart C is that the Dow has a strong tendency to sell at or above inflation-adjusted Book Value (liquidating value). Notice that in most years the solid bars representing the Dow have been above the line representing inflation-adjusted Book Value (liquidating value).

There you have it. The Dow is a bargain at its current price level. It is as simple as that. But what can we say about the future?

It is quite clear that the value of the Dow will continue to

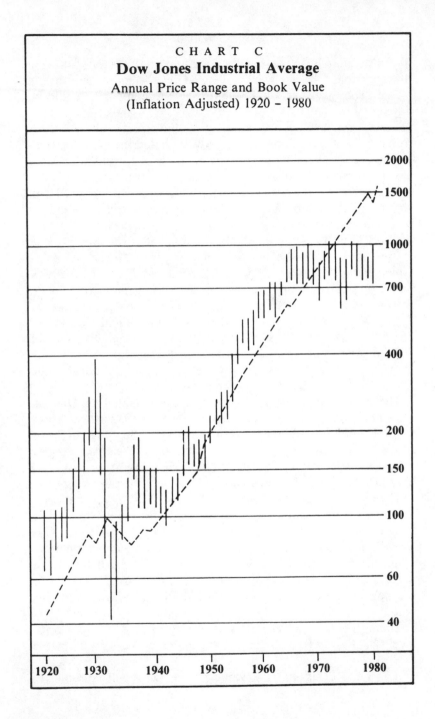

CHART C
Dow Jones Industrial Average
Annual Price Range and Book Value
(Inflation Adjusted) 1920 – 1980

increase during the Eighties. We can say this confidently for two reasons. First, the R-Factor tells us that the Dow companies will be adding new assets out of the profits they hold back from their shareholders. These assets will increase the companies' liquidating value. The only thing the R-Factor depends on is that the Dow companies be profitable in the Eighties. This seems highly likely. In only one year since 1922 have the Dow companies, in aggregate, lost money.

The second reason we can forecast an increase in value in the Eighties is inflation. Inflation raises the value of existing assets. It is easy to underestimate the effect of even single-digit inflation. What will a $1 asset be worth in nine years if inflation proceeds at 8 percent, assuming the value of the asset just keeps pace with inflation? The answer is that it will double. You can see this in Table V.

TABLE V

Value of an Asset Worth $1 at 8% Inflation if Asset's Value Keeps Pace with Inflation

YEAR	VALUE
1	$1.08
2	1.17
3	1.26
4	1.36
5	1.47
6	1.59
7	1.71
8	1.85
9	2.00

By combining the effects of the R-Factor and inflation, it is possible to estimate the Dow's liquidating value at the end of the Eighties. By 1989, we estimate that the inflation-adjusted Book Value (liquidating value) of the Dow will be approximately 3,150. This is double the Dow's current inflation-adjusted Book Value of 1,575. Such a doubling would be in line with the behavior of the Dow's inflation-adjusted Book Value (liquidating value) in the Seventies.

In our calculation, we assumed an inflation rate of 8 percent. This is slightly more than the average rate of inflation the United States experienced in the 1970s. The 8 percent assumption is well within the range of estimates by economists for inflation in the Eighties. A higher assumed rate of inflation would have made the numbers even more dramatic. A lower rate would not upset our forecast, as will be demonstrated shortly.

Based on an inflation-adjusted Book Value (liquidating value) of 3,150 on the Dow in 1989, the Dow should sell for at least 95 percent of this figure, even during a pessimistic market. This yields a forecast level of 3,000 on the Dow. This is a conservative forecast based on the fact that the Dow, as we have seen, has a strong tendency to sell *at or above* inflation-adjusted Book Value (liquidating value).

KEY POINTS

1.||Historically, the Dow has ultimately reflected its liquidating value.
2.||At present, the Dow's price in relation to liquidating value is nearly as low as it was in the Great Depression.
3.||We estimate that the Dow's liquidating value will double from the present 1,575 to 3,150 by 1989. This increase will be caused by the combined effects of the R-Factor and inflation.
4.||Based on historical relationships, the Dow should sell for at least 95 percent of its liquidating value. This yields a projected Dow of 3,000 by 1989.

CHAPTER 6
ANOTHER WAY TO DOW 3000

TWO MEN WENT into the country on a hunting trip. They noticed that a certain piece of land seemed to have a lot of birds on it, so they stopped to see if the owner would let them hunt there. The owner, a farmer, said that they could hunt on his land for nothing. However, if they wanted to use his bird dog, Secretary, it would cost them $50. One of the men responded:

"Fifty dollars is a lot of money for the use of a dog for a few hours."

The farmer replied:

"Secretary is the best bird dog in the country. Take it or leave it."

Curious about the abilities of the dog, the two men paid the $50 and set off hunting. Secretary proved to be worth every penny of the money. He led the hunters to the best spots, he flushed out the birds, and he retrieved them expertly. They couldn't have asked for a better dog.

A month later the same two men drove up to the farmer and asked if they could use Secretary again. The farmer replied:

"It'll cost you one hundred dollars to use Secretary."

One of the men said:

"But it was only fifty dollars a month ago. Why the increase?"

The farmer responded:

"I charge everyone who knows Secretary's ability one hundred dollars. I charged you only fifty dollars the first time because that's the most I figured I could get you to pay for a dog you didn't know."

The two men grumbled, but they paid the $100 and once again Secretary proved he was worth every penny.

A month later the two men went to the same farmer and asked if they could use Secretary again. This time the farmer said:

"You can use Secretary, but the charge will be only five dollars."

The two men looked at each other and then both said at the same time:

"Why only five dollars?"

The farmer replied:

"Last week I let two strangers use the dog. They got confused and kept calling him Executive . . . and now all the dog does is sit on his bottom and bark orders all day."

Just as the farmer's bird dog had two values, one as Secretary and another as Executive, there are also two ways to value a company—dead or alive.

In the previous chapters, we examined what a company was worth dead. We saw that inflation-adjusted Book Value is an approximate measure of the liquidating value of a company. And we saw that stock prices tend to reflect inflation-adjusted Book Value, because the shareholders always have the option of liquidating the company. They retain the right to sell off all of the company's assets, pay off its liabilities, and pocket the difference.

Now let's turn to the opposite question. What is a company worth alive? Imagine for a moment that you have found on your front doorstep a green metal box in the shape of a cube one foot on each side. The box is light and appears harmless, so you take it inside. Upon examining the box, you notice a small label that says: "This machine will produce $100 cash per week forever." Thinking it is a practical joke, you place the box in a corner and forget about it.

A few days later, however, your attention is attracted to the box by a whirring noise emanating from it. As you approach the box, out pops a crisp $100 bill. Again suspecting a joke, you take the $100 bill to the bank, where you are informed that it is genuine. Rushing home, you are all set to dismantle the box when you notice the label: "Any attempt to open, X-ray, or examine the inside of this box by any means will cause it to destroy itself. Made in Krypton."

Remembering the fairy tale about the goose that laid the golden eggs, you decide to leave the machine alone. Each week, however, the machine produces a crisp, genuine $100 bill without fail. After this has gone on for twenty years or so, you are convinced that the box will indeed perform this way forever. However, at this point, you need a lot of money for a business deal, and $100 a week is not sufficient. So you decide to sell the box. How much can you sell the box for?

Assume that the box has no novelty or scientific value and that its parts are inexpensive. In other words, the box will be sold solely on the basis that it will produce $100 a week forever. What is it worth?

When presented with this problem, many people respond that the value of the box is infinite. They reason that the box will produce $5,200 a year forever. Since $5,200 a year times an infinite number of years equals an infinite number of dollars, the box must have an infinite value. The conclusion that is reached by this line of reasoning is that the box is worth more than all the money in the world. Even the King of Saudi Arabia could not afford it.

However, before you set an infinite price tag on the box, consider this fact. If long-term interest rates are 10 percent, a person could invest $52,000 in a very long-term government bond and guarantee himself $5,200 income each year for a very long time. For practical purposes, the $52,000 in government bonds would behave in the same manner as the green box. Both would produce an income of $5,200 a year. Even when the bond matures a long time in the future, its owner would receive back $52,000, which he could again invest. He could keep reinvesting the $52,000 and receive an income forever. We will assume that a person will always be able to reinvest at 10 percent when the bond matures. This is unrealistic, but it simplifies our example.

Given the assumptions we have made, it is difficult to see how the green box could sell for more than $52,000. Remember, we are assuming that the box has no novelty or scientific value, and that it is being priced solely on the fact that it will produce $5,200 a year forever. Why, for example, would someone pay $100,000 for the box? If he did purchase the box for this amount, he would still receive only $5,200 a year from it. Yet the same $100,000 invested in bonds at 10 percent would pay him almost twice as much per year ($10,000). Given this choice, the rational person would invest in the bonds. Using a similar argument for other possible prices, it is clear that the most a rational investor would pay for the box, given our assumptions, would be $52,000. At this price, the income he could get from bonds would be the same as he could get from the box.

Let's change one assumption slightly. Let's assume that long-term government bonds now and in the future will yield only 5 percent. In other words, interest rates have gone down. What would the price of the box be now? Would an investor still pay $52,000 for it? Well, if the investor put the $52,000 into bonds at 5 percent, he would get only $2,600 per year. On the other hand, he would get $5,200 from the box. A rational investor would clearly be willing to buy the box for $52,000. It would give him twice as much income per year as he could get from the same amount invested in the bond market. It works out that with government bonds at 5 percent, the most an investor would pay for the box is $104,000. The reason is that $104,000 invested in bonds at 5 percent would give the investor $5,200 per year—the same amount he would get from the box.

All this arithmetic leads to a very simple conclusion. When interest rates go down, the price of income-producing assets should go up, and vice versa. Notice that when interest rates went from 10 to 5 percent the price of the box went from $52,000 to $104,000. This is a very important point, which we shall come back to later. It is so important that we are going to repeat it and italicize it. *When interest rates go down, the price of income-producing assets should go up, and vice versa.*

Now let's go back to our original case in which we found the box to be worth a maximum of $52,000. If we assume that the price of the box is $52,000, we can quantify the relationship between the price of the box and the income (earnings) it produces. We can say that the box's price is ten times income (earnings). This was derived by dividing its price ($52,000) by its income ($5,200).

This ratio of price to income is commonly referred to as the Price/Earnings Ratio. As the name implies, it is computed by dividing price by earnings. The Price/Earnings Ratio in our example is $\dfrac{52{,}000 \text{ (price)}}{5{,}200 \text{ (earnings)}} = 10.$

In our example, the green box paid out the entire amount that is produced. As we have seen, this is not true in the stock market. Companies pay out only a part of their earnings. They hold back the other part. Nevertheless, since the entire amount of the earnings does belong to the stockholder and could theoretically be paid out in full, it is the custom in the stock market to use a Price/Earnings Ratio for valuation purposes.

Price/Earnings Ratios are very handy items in the stock market. They are so handy that many newspapers print them for each stock each day. Once we know the earnings that a stock will produce, we can compute the stock's price by multiplying the earnings by a suitable Price/Earnings Ratio. We can use an equation of the following form:

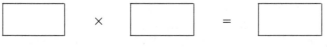

| EARNINGS | PRICE/EARNINGS RATIO | PRICE |

All that is necessary is to fill in the first two boxes with appropriate numbers, and we can compute a price.

In our green box example, the equation would look like this:

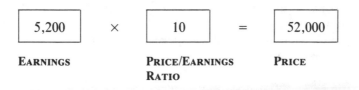

| 5,200 | × | 10 | = | 52,000 |

| EARNINGS | PRICE/EARNINGS RATIO | PRICE |

We can use this same process to price the Dow Jones Industrial Average. At the end of 1980, data for the Dow would look like this when fitted into our equation:

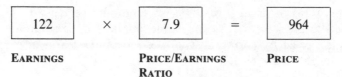

| 122 | × | 7.9 | = | 964 |

EARNINGS   **PRICE/EARNINGS**   **PRICE**
                  RATIO

The equation reflects the fact that the Dow earned $122 in 1980, that it had a 7.9 Price/Earnings Ratio, and that its closing price was 964. All of these numbers are known because we are considering past history. But what about the future? What will this equation look like for the Dow in 1989?

To project a price for the Dow in 1989, we must first estimate the numbers to be entered in the first two boxes—the earnings box and the Price/Earnings Ratio box. Let's consider the earnings box first.

In 1980, the Dow earned $122. If we experience 8 percent a year inflation in the Eighties, these earnings should double to $244. Why?

As we saw in the previous chapter, 8 percent inflation will cause the price of an asset to double in nine years. It will do exactly the same thing to consumer prices. If consumers are paying twice as much for products and services, it means that the companies providing those items are taking in twice as much money in sales. If profit margins (percentage of the sales dollar that ends up as profit) remain the same, and we see no reason to assume they will change, a doubling of sales will necessarily mean a doubling of earnings.

Thus if the United States experiences 8 percent inflation during the Eighties, the earnings of the Dow should at least double. This doubling is simply the effect of inflation. Such a result is not unreasonable in the light of past experience. In the 1970s, the consumer price index increased 104 percent. Earnings of the Dow companies increased 118 percent. We now have the first number in our equation. $244 is entered in the earnings box.

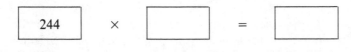

| 244 | × | | = | |

EARNINGS   **PRICE/EARNINGS**   **PRICE OF**
                  RATIO   **1989 DOW**

It should be emphasized that we are not assuming that each year the Dow's earnings will increase by exactly 8 percent. In some years of poor business conditions, it is likely that earnings will increase by less than 8 percent and may actually decline. But these subpar years should be offset by other better-than-average years with the overall result that the Dow will earn $244 in 1989. In the Seventies the Dow increased its earnings 118 percent in spite of recessions in 1970 and 1974.

The question now is: What Price/Earnings Ratio do we use in the equation? Over the last sixty years, the average Price/Earnings Ratio on the Dow has been approximately 14. If we consider just the post–World War II period, we get a similar result. In the thirty-six years since World War II, the Price/Earnings Ratio on the Dow has ranged from a high of 22.9 in 1961 to a low of 6.2 in 1974. The average of this postwar high and postwar low Price/Earnings Ratio is also approximately 14. By 1989, the Price/Earnings Ratio on the Dow should be back in the area of its historical mean: 14.

Price/Earnings Ratios, in one sense, can be thought of as measures of the confidence that investors have in the outlook for common stocks. On the same day, a medical-technology stock may have a Price/Earnings Ratio of 40 while a steel stock may have a Price/Earnings Ratio of 3. The reason for this wide discrepancy is that investors are much more optimistic about the prospects for the medical-technology stock than they are for the steel stock.

What applies to individual stocks also applies to the stock market as a whole. When we project that the Price/Earnings Ratio on the Dow will return to 14 by the end of the decade, we are really assuming that by that time investor confidence will have moved from its currently very depressed state back to at least an average level. Historically, a Price/Earnings Ratio of 14 represents an average level of confidence in the outlook for the stocks composing the Dow.

What factors will cause this rebound in confidence? There are several. Our list is by no means exhaustive:

1. Recent changes in the capital gains tax rates have made common stocks much more desirable tax-wise.

2. As investors become more aware of the enormous buildup

in asset values behind common stocks, they will recognize the great bargain that the stock market offers.

3. Competition from high interest rates will lessen as investors increasingly recognize the dangers of long-term bonds in an inflationary economy. As this is being written, every straight bond (those without special features) ever issued is selling for less than its original issue price. Investors will also learn that very high short-term interest rates on money market funds and other instruments can evaporate very quickly, leaving them stuck with low yields.

4. Psychologically, there is a natural tendency for extreme mood swings to return to normal. Human nature seems to resist being perpetually optimistic or pessimistic. We will discuss these factors at greater length in succeeding chapters.

Inserting 14 into the Price/Earnings Ratio box allows us to complete the equation and arrive at an estimate of the Dow for 1989.

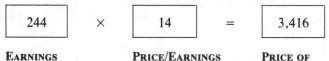

244	×	14	=	3,416
EARNINGS		PRICE/EARNINGS RATIO		PRICE OF 1989 DOW

Multiply it out for yourself: 244 times 14 equals 3,416. Rounded to the lowest thousand to allow for possible contingencies gives a projection of Dow 3,000 by 1989.

Congratulations! You have survived the two most difficult chapters in the book. Everything is much easier from here on.

KEY POINTS

1.‖ The Price/Earnings Ratio is the ratio of price to earnings. It is computed by dividing the price of a stock by its earnings.

2.‖ The following equation can be used to forecast a price for the Dow in 1989:

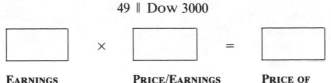

EARNINGS	×	**PRICE/EARNINGS** **RATIO**	=	**PRICE OF** **1989 DOW**

3.‖ By 1989, the Dow's Price/Earnings Ratio should be back to its historical average of 14.

4.‖ By 1989, the Dow's earnings should double from their present 122 to 244 as a result of 8 percent inflation in the Eighties.

5.‖ Filling in the boxes in our equation results in a projected Dow of 3,416, which we have rounded to 3,000 to allow for contingencies.

244	×	14	=	3,416
EARNINGS		**PRICE/EARNINGS** **RATIO**		**PRICE OF** **1989 DOW**

CHAPTER 7
THE GREAT CRASH AND THE SAFETY NET

ALBERT EINSTEIN IS reputed to have walked into a classroom at Princeton one day and found a group of graduate students grappling with a complex mathematical problem written on the blackboard. Einstein saw the problem on the blackboard and stood looking at it for several minutes. He then walked over and wrote a few numbers representing the answer under the problem.

From the back of the room, one of the students remarked to Einstein:

"Professor Einstein, isn't there another way to solve that problem?"

Einstein stared at the blackboard for several minutes. Then he replied:

"That's right. There is another way to solve it."

Einstein then proceeded to erase the first answer and write the exact same answer in its place. The students were, of course, dumbfounded, since in neither case had Einstein shown the intermediate steps he had used in solving the problem. But his prestige was such that no one challenged the fact that there were indeed two ways to solve the problem.

The reason we have gone into such detail regarding our forecast of Dow 3,000 is that we wanted you to see exactly how it was computed, including the intermediate steps, so that you could judge for yourself whether it was reasonable or not. We didn't want to leave you in the position of Einstein's pupils, who had to take the answer on faith.

One of the major problems with Wall Street is its tendency to concentrate almost exclusively on short-term developments. There is an overemphasis on what a company will earn next quarter or on what the economy will do next year. It is this excessive concern with what is going to happen in the short run that causes many investors to miss out on the really big moves in the stock market—the moves that create great fortunes.

Losing sight of the long term, investors tend to become fearful when the stock market declines, and they are reluctant to buy stocks. They ignore the tremendous opportunities that these declines can offer, particularly if the decline has taken stocks below their liquidating value. By standing back and looking at the underlying mechanisms that generate long-term stock prices, it is possible to overcome this myopia. This is what we are attempting to do in this book.

So far we have argued that liquidating value is a basic influence on long-term stock prices. We have said that liquidating value is important because stockholders always retain the right to sell off a company's assets, pay off its debts, and pocket the difference. As a measure of liquidating value, we used the inflation-adjusted Book Value of the Dow Average. We saw that over the long run, the Dow's price has been clearly influenced by the rise in its liquidating value. We also saw that it was possible to estimate what the Dow's liquidating value would be in 1989 by taking account of the fact that corporations retain a part of their profits and by taking account of probable future inflation. Using historical tendencies, we were then able to forecast a price for the Dow in 1989 from this estimated liquidating value.

We have also argued that earnings are another substantial influence on long-term stock prices. They are significant because they represent the economic return that the companies are generating for their shareholders. By making an assumption about future inflation, we were able to forecast that the Dow's earnings would double by 1989. We further argued that the Price/Earnings Ratio of the Dow will have returned to its historical average by 1989. Multiplying these two elements together, we arrived at a forecast for the Dow in 1989. The fascinating thing about the two different approaches that we have examined is that they both project a Dow in excess of 3,000 by 1989.

In both of the approaches we used an assumed rate of inflation of 8 percent per year during the Eighties. Based upon current estimates of economists and the actual experience of the United States in the Seventies, this appears to be a reasonable assumption. In the 1970s, the United States experienced inflation at the average rate of 7.5 percent per year. If inflation is substantially higher than 8 percent, that will only increase assets and earnings even faster and produce a Dow of 4,000 or 5,000. If we experience a hyperinflation as in Germany in 1920–23, we could see a Dow of several million. We will discuss this possibility at greater length in a later chapter.

But what if inflation averages only 1 or 2 percent? Will that upset the forecast? The answer is no. The reason is that with low inflation we would have much lower interest rates in the bond market and thus less competition for stocks.

A rule of thumb in the bond market is that bonds should yield 3 percent over the expected rate of inflation. Thus, if investors expect 8 percent inflation, we would anticipate seeing bond yields around 11 percent. If, however, investors expect only 2 percent inflation, then we would anticipate bond yields in the 5 percent area. In the early Sixties, when inflation was very low, 5 percent was, in fact, the yield on many bonds.

Remember the point that we repeated twice and even italicized in the last chapter: *When interest rates go down, the price of income-producing assets should go up, and vice versa.* Well, common stocks are income-producing assets. They pay dividends. And they are influenced by declining interest rates in the same way that other income-producing assets are. Stock prices should go up dramatically if long-term interest rates drop substantially. Remember how the price of the green box reacted to a decline in the assumed interest rate. It went from $52,000 to $104,000. Thus if inflation is brought under control, stocks should do very well indeed because of the low interest rates that would prevail in the bond market.

But what if inflation accelerates and interest rates go higher? Doesn't the same principle work the other way? Won't higher interest rates cause stocks to drop? The answer to this question is yes and no. In the short term, dramatically higher interest rates would cause the stock market to drop. We have seen this response occur in the summer of 1981. In the long term, however, higher interest rates should not have a sustained negative effect. The reason is that higher inflation would accompany permanently higher interest rates. And higher inflation would in turn cause the liquidating values of corporations to increase that much faster. It is the increase in liquidating values that will ultimately carry the stock market much higher—regardless of what interest rates do. Higher interest rates can only postpone the inevitable stock market explosion. They cannot permanently prevent it.

Liquidating values, in effect, provide a safety net for stock prices. In the late Sixties, stock prices were well above liquidating values. There was nothing to impede a downward fall in their price. Stock prices were like a trapeze artist at the circus soaring through the air, high above the safety net. When interest rates increased dramatically in the late Sixties and early Seventies, the short-term effect of interest rates operated in full force and stock prices crashed. The trapeze artist fell all the way down to the safety net and then deep into it. However, once the trapeze artist is already in the safety net, it is difficult for him to fall much farther. That is the position the stock market is in at the present time. It is well into the safety net provided by liquidating values. That is not to say that stock prices can't temporarily decline further. After all, a safety net is elastic. But the farther prices sink into the net, the more resistance they will experience and the greater will be the ultimate rebound.

Many people are not aware of how far stock prices actually crashed in the Seventies. The trapeze artist took a tremendous fall. The reason is that the magnitude of the drop was concealed by inflation. However, *in terms of purchasing power, the stock market decline in the Seventies was almost as large as that experienced in the Great Crash of 1929.* Chart D is a chart of the Dow in terms of both current and constant dollars.

The constant-dollar line reflects the movement of the Dow in terms of purchasing power. Note the tremendous drop that has occurred since the late Sixties. Compare this drop with the one

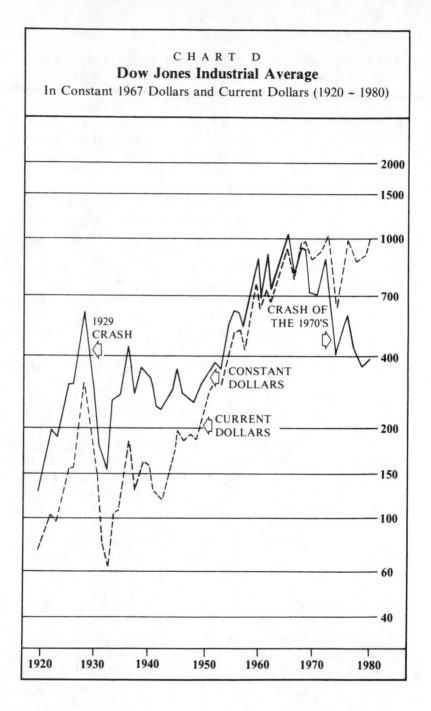

C H A R T   D
Dow Jones Industrial Average
In Constant 1967 Dollars and Current Dollars (1920 – 1980)

that occurred in 1929. They are comparable in magnitude. Most investors haven't noticed the crash because, in terms of current dollars, the Dow has stayed essentially level in price. Note the apparent plateau in the Dow shown in its current-dollar price on Chart D.

The Great Crash of 1929 created tremendous values. Those investors who purchased stocks in the early Thirties and held them were rewarded with gigantic increases. We believe that the crash of the Seventies has created a similar situation. Tremendous values are now available in the stock market. Investors who purchase stocks in the early Eighties should be rewarded with a dramatic advance.

KEY POINTS

1. ‖ If the rate of inflation in the Eighties is greater than the 8 percent we assumed, it will mean that the Dow's earnings and liquidating value will grow at an even faster rate, and a Dow of 4,000 or 5,000 becomes likely.

2. ‖ When interest rates go down, the price of income-producing assets should go up, and vice versa.

3. ‖ This principle explains why, if the rate of inflation in the Eighties is substantially less than our assumed 8 percent, the stock market should do well. Lower inflation will mean lower interest rates. And lower interest rates mean higher stock prices, since stocks are income-producing assets (they pay dividends).

4. ‖ Liquidating values now provide a safety net for stock prices. Stock prices can decline under the influence of dramatically higher interest rates, but they will encounter increasing resistance as they fall deeper into the safety net of liquidating values. The tension generated by the stretching of the safety net will cause the ultimate rebound to be that much greater.

5.‖In terms of purchasing power, the stock market decline in the Seventies was almost as large as that experienced in the Great Crash of 1929. Tremendous values have been created for the long-term investor.

CHAPTER 8
ACTIONS SPEAK LOUDER THAN WORDS

TWO NINE-YEAR-OLD boys were arguing about how far a football could be kicked. One boy, Johnny, was very proud of his father and was prone to exaggerate his father's abilities. His father had been on the football team in college. Johnny claimed that his father could kick a football the length of a football field in the air. He said that he and his father frequently played touch football on the high school football field, and that many times his father had kicked the ball the length of the field.

Bobby, the other boy, very vehemently denied that this was possible. He said that he had seen many football games on TV, and that he had never seen even the best punters or place kickers on professional teams kick a ball that far. The two boys went round and round on the subject as only nine-year-olds can until Bobby finally said:

"I'll bet you my allowance against your allowance that your father can't kick a football the length of the field in the air. Put your money where your mouth is. Put up or shut up."

Johnny, knowing that he had exaggerated, didn't accept the bet. Fortunately for him, Bobby's mother called for Bobby to come home for dinner, and Johnny was saved further embarrassment.

This story very clearly illustrates the principle that statements which a person is willing to back with money tend to be more trustworthy than ones not backed by money. The same principle applies in the stock market. Opinions which knowledgeable people are willing to back with substantial sums of cash are more likely to be worthy of serious consideration than opinions which are not backed with money. In other words, pay attention to what people do, not to what they say.

If we examine what the managements of many American corporations have been doing in the last few years, it is quite obvious that they have concluded that stocks are generally undervalued. And they have been willing to back their conclusions with billions of dollars. Below is a partial list of major corporations which have repurchased shares in themselves since 1978. In a repurchase, the corporation uses company funds to buy back its own stock held by shareholders. The effect is to shrink the number of shares outstanding in the company.

> Citicorp
> Dow Chemical
> Georgia-Pacific
> Gulf & Western
> IBM
> Levi Strauss
> Marriott
> NCR
> Norton Simon
> PepsiCo
> Schering-Plough
> Sears, Roebuck
> Standard Oil of Indiana
> Texaco
> Times Mirror
> Travelers
> Weyerhaeuser
> Winn-Dixie Stores

The list includes several companies that are noted for their extremely astute management. When IBM buys back $400 million of its own stock, its management is, in effect, saying that it thinks it can make more money for the shareholders by buying IBM stock than it can in its computer business. This is probably the most potent way that IBM management can say that it believes that IBM stock is undervalued.

It is highly significant that stock repurchases have been at all-time record levels in recent years. In the late Sixties, when stocks were greatly overvalued, very few corporations repurchased their own shares. Corporations wouldn't be buying back their own stock if their managements didn't think that they were at bargain levels. And who is in a better position to judge whether a company is a bargain than the company's own executives? They presumably know everything there is to know about the company and its prospects. This action, by extremely savvy corporate managements, offers very strong corroboration for our thesis that stocks are undervalued.

We have asserted that stocks are generally selling below liquidating value. If this is true, one would think that there would be a lot of companies being liquidated. Yet in the news we don't hear about many companies voluntarily going out of business and distributing the net proceeds to their shareholders. Why? The reason is that companies are, in fact, being liquidated—but in a disguised form. Instead of selling off the assets piecemeal, paying off the liabilities, and distributing the net proceeds to the shareholders, the companies are simply being sold in their entirety for an amount which approximates liquidating value. This process occurs under the name of merger, acquisition, or takeover. That's why it hasn't been more obvious. Following is a list of just a few of the companies that have been acquired or merged since 1978:

Ampex
Bache
Beech Aircraft
CIT Financial
Congoleum
Crocker National
Dart Industries
Elha
Foremost-McKesson
Hobart
Houston Oil

Howard Johnson
Kennecott
Liggett Group
Pullman
Reliance Electric
Reserve Oil
Shearson Loeb Rhoades
Southwestern Life
Studebaker-Worthington
Teleprompter

The interesting thing about these mergers and acquisitions is the price paid in relation to market price. W. T. Grimm & Co., 135 South LaSalle Street, Chicago, IL 60603, keeps track of the statistics on all mergers and acquisitions in the United States and for a small fee will mail you a summary of each year's acquisition activity.

In 1979 and 1980, W. T. Grimm & Co.'s figures show that the average acquisition price was 50 percent above market. In other words, if a company's stock was selling in the open market at $50 per share, the acquiring company, on average, actually paid $75 per share.

Why would companies pay 50 percent above current market price to acquire another company? The answer is that they think they are getting good value for their money. They realize that even after paying a 50 percent premium they are still getting assets at less than it would cost to build those same assets from scratch. These figures are in line with the estimate we made in Chapter 5 that the Dow stocks are currently selling for almost 45 percent less than their liquidating value (their inflation-adjusted Book Value).

Another interesting statistic that appears in W. T. Grimm & Co.'s summary reports is the Price/Earnings Ratios that are being paid in these acquisitions. The average Price/Earnings Ratio paid was 14.3 in 1979 and 15.2 in 1980. Do these numbers sound familiar? Remember our assumption that the Price/Earnings Ratio on the Dow would be 14 in 1989. Price/Earnings Ratios of this amount are already being paid in the acquisition market.

It should be emphasized that these acquisitions and takeovers are not an isolated phenomenon. In terms of the dollar amounts involved, they have been at record levels in the last two years. Just the top twenty acquisitions, in terms of size, amounted to almost $34 billion in 1979 and 1980. So we are not talking about insignificant amounts of money.

Judging from their actions, it is quite obvious that many corporate managements clearly believe that stocks are undervalued. And they are backing their belief with billions of dollars. We think these actions offer substantial evidence of our contention that common stocks in the United States represent exceptional bargains at the present time.

Further corroboration of our thesis comes from John Templeton. Mr. Templeton is considered one of the best investment managers in the world. His Templeton Growth Fund, Ltd., has had, over the last twenty-five years, the best record of any mutual fund in the world. $1,000 invested in 1954 in the Templeton Growth Fund, Ltd., would have grown to $268,000 by 1980. The opinion of a man who has compiled such a documented record of success for so long a period of time deserves a great deal of respect.

John Templeton gave early evidence of an extraordinary talent for investments. One day in 1939, he walked into the office of a major brokerage firm and placed an order to purchase $100 worth of every listed stock selling at $1 a share or less. The total bill for these purchases came to $10,000, an amount John Templeton had borrowed. Approximately four years later, the stocks were sold for $40,000.

The reason John Templeton placed his unusual order was that he was convinced that stocks were greatly undervalued as a result of the Depression and that the extremely low-priced stocks were the greatest bargains. He reasoned that the war in Europe would stimulate the American economy and that all stocks would rise, including the "cats and dogs" (extremely low-priced stocks).

Over the years, Mr. Templeton has followed the strategy of buying the best bargains among the universe of stocks available. In his search for bargains, he has not confined himself to the United States stock market. He looks for bargains all over the world. In the late Sixties and early Seventies, the bulk of his fund's assets were not invested in the United States stock market, which he considered to be overvalued. Instead, for the most part they were invested in Japan and other countries.

Now Mr. Templeton is investing the bulk of the money he manages in the United States stock market. He believes that the best bargains in common stocks are to be found in America. For the past few years, he has indicated that he believes that there is a better than even chance the Dow will have reached 3,000 by the end of the Eighties. In May 1981, he reiterated this opinion in an interview with Louis Rukeyser on the *Wall Street Week* television program.

As far as we are aware, Mr. Templeton was the first investment manager to publicly predict a Dow of 3,000 by the end of the Eighties. He has backed his opinion with a great deal of money. Mr. Templeton had invested $667 million of his two mutual funds' assets in United States common stocks as of January 31, 1981.

KEY POINTS

1. ‖ In recent years, major corporations such as IBM and Citicorp have been buying back stock in themselves. They have done this because they realize that their stocks represent great bargains at the repurchase price.
2. ‖ With stocks generally below liquidating value, it would be expected that many companies would be liquidated. This is, in fact, what is occurring at the present time in the form of acquisitions, mergers, and takeovers. Companies are being sold in their entirety for an amount that approximates their liquidating values.
3. ‖ The actual prices paid to buy companies in their entirety have been averaging 50 percent over the market price of the companies' shares. The purchase prices have been at Price/Earnings Ratios averaging 14 to 15.

4.‖One of the world's leading investment managers
has recently reiterated on the *Wall Street Week*
television program his belief that there is a better
than even chance that the Dow will be at 3,000 by
the end of the Eighties.

CHAPTER 9
MONEY: THE FUEL

ONEY IS TO the stock market
what jet fuel is to the modern air-
liner. Without an adequate supply
of money, the stock market simply will not fly. No matter how
undervalued stocks may be, if potential purchasers do not have
the money to bid their price up, stocks will languish. History has
shown that it takes an ample supply of money to sustain higher
prices in the stock market.

Is there sufficient money available to sustain a Dow of 3,000?
The answer is unequivocally yes. By fostering inflation, the government has seen to that. *More money has been created in the
United States in the last fifteen years than has been created in
all prior years combined since the adoption of the Constitution.*
If the government could manufacture oil with the same ease that
it manufactures money, the United States would have such vast
quantities of oil that it could sell it to OPEC for less than one
cent a barrel.

Part of the problem is that there is no check on the amount of
money the government can spend and, therefore, has to create.
Harry Truman was well aware of this fact when he appeared at
Yale University some years ago to give a speech. Afterward, one
of the undergraduates came up to Mr. Truman with a question:

"Mr. Truman, how do I start in politics?"

Truman, thinking of the amount it was costing the student's
father to pay his way through the Ivy League school, replied with
a wry smile:

"You've already started. You're spending someone else's
money."

One gets the general impression that prices have always been rising in the United States, and that inflation has always been with us. We read about full-course steak dinners costing 50 cents at the turn of the century, and it is easy to conclude that a steak dinner must have been even cheaper a hundred years earlier. Yet such is not the case. Large-scale continuing inflation is a relatively new development in the United States dating back only to World War II.

Chart E is a chart of prices in the United States from the adoption of the Constitution to the present. The distinguishing feature of the chart is that the price line is essentially flat until World War II. Prices in the Depression were no higher than they were in 1812. There were spurts of inflation around the War of 1812, the Civil War, and World War I, but prices receded after these spurts.

Inflation did not get a real start until just prior to World War II. At this time, the government first began running massive deficits to counteract the Depression and then to finance the war. These deficits were funded, in effect, by creating money. This creation of excessive amounts of money began our current inflation. It has continued to this day as a result of the fact that government finds it easier to create new money than to balance the budget. It is no coincidence that the ever increasing federal budget deficits have been accompanied by accelerating inflation.

The government has attempted to divert attention from its role as the root cause of inflation by blaming business, labor, the weather, OPEC, and anything else that is handy, but fewer and fewer Americans are accepting these explanations. People are painfully coming to the realization that the federal government itself is the fundamental cause of our inflation.

In the last few years, inflation has put enormous sums of additional liquid assets in the hands of individuals. By the end of 1980, households in the United States possessed $1,644 billion in liquid assets (currency, checking and savings accounts, and money market funds). Written in an equivalent way, this is 1.6 trillion dollars, more than three times the amount that individuals had only twelve years earlier. The result is an enormous reservoir of potential purchasing power available to the stock market. The Board of Governors of the Federal Reserve System publishes a very interesting set of statistics called *Flow of Funds*.

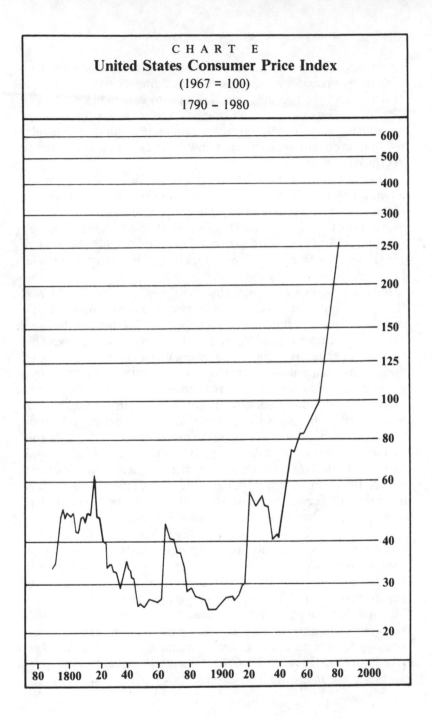

CHART E
United States Consumer Price Index
(1967 = 100)
1790 – 1980

These statistics trace the course of various financial assets through the economy. They are interesting because they can be used to estimate the potential magnitude of the rise in stock values that could occur in the 1980s, based on the amount of liquid assets available.

Data in *Flow of Funds* reveal that the total value of all stocks in the United States was $120 billion in 1949. At the same time, individuals had $135 billion in liquid assets. It thus took about $1 in liquid assets to support $1 in stock values.

By 1968, individuals had $503 billion in liquid assets, and the total value of all stock was $1,034 billion. At this point, $1 in liquid assets was able to support $2 in stock values.

In 1980, we were back to essentially the same position that prevailed in 1949, when it took $1 in liquid assets to support $1 in stock values. At the end of 1980, individuals had $1,644 billion in liquid assets, and the total value of all stock was $1,573 billion.

What can we expect in the future? If the United States experiences 8 percent inflation in the Eighties, the liquid assets of individuals should grow at least at the same rate as inflation. This means that household liquid assets would double, reaching at least $3,288 billion. Such growth in liquid assets would be somewhat less than what occurred in the 1970s. In the Seventies, liquid assets actually grew at an 11 percent per year rate.

Based on the relationship between liquid assets and stock values that we just discussed, $3,288 billion in liquid assets in 1989 would support a total value of all stocks of one to two times this amount (1 × $3,288 billion = $3,288 billion or 2 × $3,288 billion = $6,576 billion in total stock values respectively). These total stock values translate into a doubling or quadrupling of the present amount of $1,573 billion in total stock values. Our forecast of a tripling of stock prices falls in the middle of this range.

The numbers make it quite clear that individuals alone have sufficient money to drive the Dow to 3,000. But they are not the only category of investors in the American stock market. Pension funds have become a dominant force in the investment world. They now account for more than half of the dollar value of trading on the New York Stock Exchange. Pension funds have enormous new inflows of cash each year which have to be invested. And these inflows are increasing at a dramatic rate. In the last ten years, the amount of investable cash flowing annually into pension funds has increased more than 3.5 times to $47 billion in 1980. Over the next nine years, if pension funds invest just one-third of their investable cash inflow in the market, they will be investing over $200 billion in new money in the market.

To get an idea of the magnitude of the money that pension funds have to invest, consider that the dollar value of all stocks traded in a day in the United States is approximately $3 billion. As these pension funds attempt to invest even a part of their huge cash inflows in the market, it will be like an elephant jumping into a small swimming pool. The water level (stock prices) will have to rise.

Another source of cash to sustain a stock market rise is the overseas investor. The United States remains by far the largest, most liquid market for securities in the world. The United States also has a strong tradition of private property and free enterprise. These characteristics should serve to attract foreign money in a politically unstable world. Britain recently allowed its pension funds to invest overseas. These funds have assets of over $100 billion. The OPEC countries have accumulated large sums of investable cash. If even a relatively small portion of OPEC's money flowed into the American stock market, the results would be spectacular. The recent novel *Green Monday,* by Michael Thomas, explored this possibility in fascinating detail.

It is quite clear that there is ample money available to fuel a dramatic rise in the stock market. But what will cause this money to flow into the market? The answer to this question lies in taxes, as we shall see.

KEY POINTS

1. ‖ There is ample money in the United States to fuel a rise in the Dow to 3,000. More money has been created in the United States in the last fifteen years than has been created in all prior years combined since the adoption of the Constitution.

2.‖Individuals alone, by 1989, will have sufficient liquid assets to support anywhere from a doubling to a quadrupling of total stock values.

3.‖Pension funds will have enormous sums of cash that they will have to invest in the Eighties. When they invest even a small portion of this cash into the stock market, the effect will be similar to that of an elephant jumping into a small swimming pool.

CHAPTER 10
CAPITAL GAINS: THE IGNITION

NERO WOLFE FANS will remember that around the end of the year, when Wolfe had earned several substantial fees, the fat detective was extremely reluctant to take on a new case. Archie, his right-hand man, had to use all of his guile to persuade Wolfe to accept a deserving client. Wolfe could see no point in having to endure the great hardship of using his brain to solve a crime when the government would take over nine-tenths of his fee. He would much rather play with his orchids and concoct new culinary delights. While Wolfe was a fictional character, he no doubt reflected the attitude of many real people.

It is easy to forget that from World War II to 1964 the maximum federal tax on income was 91 percent. This meant that out of every additional dollar a high-income person earned, 91 cents went to the Internal Revenue Service. It is not surprising that many creative tax shelters were devised during this period.

One of the stories that circulated through a major corporation during this era involved the company's chairman. It was the chairman's practice to play golf each week with several junior executives in order to keep in touch with what was going on at the company's lower levels. Every time the chairman hit a golf ball into the rough, he would invariably search through the underbrush to find the ball. The junior executives couldn't understand why a man earning nearly $300,000 a year was wasting his valuable time to find a $1 golf ball. Finally, one of the executives got up enough nerve to ask the chairman why he tried so hard to recover each ball. The chairman replied:

"They may be one-dollar golf balls to you fellows, but they're

70

ten-dollar golf balls to me. That's how much I have to earn before tax to pay for one of the damn things."

Exactly how much high tax rates cause people to do less work is a controversial question. High tax rates obviously caused Nero Wolfe to do less work. And they affected the behavior of the chairman of the corporation. This may sound strange, but sociologists have found that people work for a variety of reasons besides money. Some enjoy the challenge, some enjoy the friends they make, some enjoy the status their job gives, and some enjoy the structure a job gives to their lives. Thus a high tax rate may not necessarily have a dramatic effect on how much people work.

The one area of behavior where high tax rates do have a profound effect, however, is in investing. The reason people invest is to make money. There generally aren't any complicating factors such as status, friends, structure to life, etc. Given the amount of risk they are willing to take, people usually try to make as much money as they can on their investments. People are particularly interested in how much they get to keep after taxes. Thus if one form of investment is highly taxed and another form of investment is lightly taxed, investors will shift money to the lightly taxed investment.

Changes in the tax laws explain a great deal about the stock market's behavior in the twentieth century. They are the primary mechanism that triggers the flow of liquid assets into and out of the stock market. Taxes have such a crucial and often overlooked effect on the stock market that it is important to review the historical record.

In 1913, Congress passed "An Act to Reduce Tariff Duties and Provide Revenue for the Government, and for Other Purposes." While it isn't clear from the title, this is the law that imposed the income tax as we know it. An income tax had been made constitutional by the Sixteenth Amendment to the Constitution, which provides: "The Congress shall have power to lay and collect taxes on incomes, from whatever source derived, without apportionment among the several States, and without regard to any census or enumeration."

The income tax as imposed in 1913 wasn't particularly onerous. It provided for taxes of 1 to 7 percent on incomes, after an exemption of $4,000 for married couples. Adjusted for inflation, that $4,0C;) would be the equivalent of about $35,000 today. As first imposed, the tax was clearly designed to be born by the wealthy.

With America's entry into World War I, the government found itself in need of greatly expanded revenues, and it raised tax rates on income dramatically. By 1918, the top bracket was 77 percent. This was quite a jump from the low rates of just a few years earlier.

The crucially important fact about the income tax in these years is that gains from sales of assets were treated just like other income. In other words, there was no special provision for capital gains. Thus a wealthy investor who bought a stock at $50 and subsequently sold it at $100 had to pay more than three-quarters of his profit to Uncle Sam in income tax. There was clearly no incentive to invest in stocks.

In the Revenue Act of 1921, Congress made a very significant change in the tax laws. It introduced a special provision for capital gains. Congress provided that the gain from the sale of an asset would be taxed at a maximum of 12.5 percent, if the asset had been held for at least two years. This favorable treatment of capital gains created a very great incentive for the wealthy to invest in common stocks. A wealthy investor who received $100 in interest income would have had to pay $56 to the federal government in taxes, whereas if he made a $100 profit on a stock held two years he would have had to pay only $12.50. Naturally, the wealthy gravitated into the stock market.

Stock market historians have tended to ignore the role that this change in the tax laws played in fostering the great bull market of the 1920s. Yet this change undoubtedly directed large sums of money into stocks. It is no coincidence that the Revenue Act of 1921 marked the beginning of a dramatic rise in the stock market. The tax change was sufficient to begin the process that ultimately snowballed into the greatest bull market that had ever been seen.

During the Depression, the government found itself needing more money, and it substantially increased the tax brackets for the wealthy. The maximum rate was boosted first to 63 percent and then to 79 percent. In addition, capital gains taxes were substantially stiffened. For holding periods of one to two years the maximum tax on capital gains worked out to be 50 percent, and for two-to-five-year holding periods 37.8 percent.

Then, in 1942, Congress made a substantial change in the capital gains rates. It adopted a maximum tax of 25 percent on capital gains made on assets held more than six months. At the same time, Congress raised the maximum tax on ordinary income to 88 percent. These changes again created a very great incentive to invest in stocks. And, again, it was no coincidence that 1942 marked the real beginning of the great bull market that ended in the late Sixties. All during the Fifties and Sixties investors were attracted to growth stocks because they offered the best chance for capital gains. Many growth stocks had fabulous rises during this period.

The party ended, however, with the passage of the Tax Reform Act of 1969. This act boosted the maximum tax on capital gains for a wealthy investor to almost 50 percent. The incentive to invest in stocks was dramatically curtailed. This change, along with the fact that stocks were generally overvalued in the late Sixties, led to substantial stock market declines in the market in the early Seventies. Venture capital—money to finance small corporations with innovative products—dried up during this period.

In 1978, Congress again made a dramatic change in the capital gains tax. The maximum tax rate on capital gains was reduced to 28 percent. Congress had become concerned with the lack of investment in productive facilities in America. The United States was lagging behind Germany and Japan in competitive position. Congress was aware that Japan does not tax capital gains and that Germany has a very low tax on them.

With the reduction in capital gains taxes, venture capital revived. Investors were again willing to finance small corporations with innovative ideas. In addition, there was now a strong incentive to invest in stocks. Income from interest and rents was taxed at a 70 percent maximum, whereas profits on stocks held for more than one year were taxed at a maximum of 28 percent.

The tax cut passed in 1981 further reduced the capital gains tax to the present maximum of 20 percent. This is a drastic reduction from the 50 percent that prevailed just four years earlier.

If history is any guide, the recent reductions in the capital gains tax will ultimately cause a massive amount of money to flow back into stocks. And, as we have seen in Chapter 9, there are huge sums of liquid assets available to be diverted into the market.

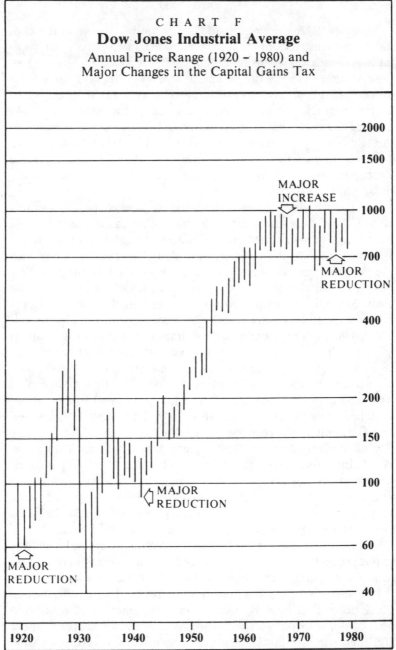

CHART F
Dow Jones Industrial Average
Annual Price Range (1920 – 1980) and
Major Changes in the Capital Gains Tax

Chart F makes very clear the impact that changes in capital gains tax rates have had on the stock market. Arrows on the chart point to the years in which significant changes were made in the rates. Note that 1921 and 1942 marked the beginning of massive stock market rises. Note also the poor performance of the market after the 1969 Tax Reform Act.

KEY POINTS

1.‖ Changes in the tax laws are a primary mechanism that regulates the flow of liquid assets into and out of the stock market.
2.‖ The raising of capital gains tax rates in 1969 was a partial cause of the stock market crash in the Seventies.
3.‖ Reductions in the capital gains tax rate in 1921 and 1942 ignited great bull markets.
4.‖ Major reductions in the capital gains tax rate were made in 1978 and 1981. We believe that these changes will ultimately ignite another great bull market.

CHAPTER 11
THE BANDWAGON EFFECT: THE AMPLIFIER

MANY YEARS AGO, a young professor of statistics from a major university found himself stuck in a small midwestern town when the train he was on broke down. Not having anything else to do, he wandered into the local bar, where he found several poker games in session. Considering himself an excellent card player because of his training in statistics, he joined one of the games. After several hands, the young professor was moderately ahead. Then he was dealt four jacks. Concealing his glee, he bet carefully, nursing the pot to a respectable size. When he called, the last person remaining in the pot, a retired farmer, laid down a hand consisting of the two and seven of spades and the three, nine, and king of hearts. Laying down his four jacks, the professor reached for the pot.

At this point, the farmer said:

"Hold it son. A zamboni beats four jacks."

Surprised, the young professor replied:

"What's a zamboni?"

The farmer pointed to a sign over the bar that said: "In this establishment a zamboni—two spades and three hearts—beats any other poker hand."

After a heated argument by the young professor, which ceased only when he was confronted by several muscular farmers, the game continued. The young professor angrily muttered under his breath, "If that's the way you want to play." Several hands later the young professor was again in a very sizable pot with the farmer. When called, the farmer laid down four queens. Triumphantly reaching for the pot, the professor laid down two spades and three hearts—a zamboni.

At this point, the farmer said:

"Son, don't you learn the rules before you play a game?"

And he pointed to the sign on the wall opposite the bar: "A zamboni may be played only once each day in this establishment."

The moral of the story, of course, is to make sure that you fully understand the rules of any game you play. Knowing what a zamboni was and how it operated was crucial to the finances of the young professor. Similarly, it is crucial to the finances of the investor in the stock market to understand "the Bandwagon Effect" and how it operates.

We define the Bandwagon Effect as the almost irresistible tendency of people to follow certain trends once they gain sufficient momentum. It applies in politics, fashion, business, hula hoops, and, most crucially, in the stock market. Once a trend gets a certain momentum, people rush to join it. They do not want to be left out. Political conventions give the most visible demonstration of this phenomenon.

Most of the time, there is nothing wrong with following the crowd. In fact, this tendency has very great survival value for the human species. It promotes shared values and attitudes and is a key ingredient in holding society together.

In the stock market, however, this tendency to follow the crowd frequently has very expensive consequences. The reason is that it leads people to buy at times when prices are greatly above underlying values—when everyone else is buying. And it leads people to sell or to ignore common stocks when prices are greatly below underlying values—when everyone else is selling or will not touch common stocks. In 1929, doctors, bus drivers, lawyers, shoeshine boys, housewives, and businessmen were all eagerly buying common stocks at a time when they were far above sustainable levels. In 1932, it was difficult to find anyone to buy stock. Even the people who had substantial amounts of cash were reluctant to buy when stocks were demonstrably selling far below underlying value.

While 1929 and 1932 are the most extreme examples of the Bandwagon Effect at work, they are not isolated cases. The Bandwagon Effect is operating almost continuously in the stock market.

Bernard Baruch, one of the greatest stock market investors of all time, was well aware of the effects of crowd psychology on the stock market. He understood that he had to insulate himself from the emotion of the moment in order to be successful. Baruch trained himself to see the true value of stocks undistorted by transient optimism or pessimism. This talent made him a multimillionaire. One of the techniques he used to attain detachment was to repeat this quotation from Schiller: "Anyone taken as an individual is tolerably sensible and reasonable—as a member of a crowd, he at once becomes a blockhead."

Baruch also frequently reread *Extraordinary Popular Delusions and the Madness of Crowds,* by Charles Mackay. Reading about earlier financial manias enabled Baruch to gain a detached perspective on the market madness of the moment. He was able to see that the crowd usually takes prices to an unsustainable level from which they ultimately fall precipitately.

Baruch found two stories in the book to be of particular value. The lesson they taught allowed him to avoid the worst part of the 1929 crash. The first was the story of the Mississippi Scheme of John Law. John Law was the son of a wealthy banker and goldsmith in Scotland. After killing a man in a duel, Law was forced to flee from Scotland. He spent the next several years frequenting gambling houses on the Continent. In Paris, he made the acquaintance of the Duke of Orleans, to whom he often expounded on his favorite topic other than gambling—public finance.

Upon the death of Louis XIV, in 1715, the Duke of Orleans became regent governing France. The Duke found business stagnant and the country on the verge of bankruptcy, because of the free spending of Louis XIV. The Duke turned to his old friend, Law, for help. Law was granted the right to establish a bank which could issue paper money. The bank was an immediate success, and business revived with the added purchasing power generated by Law's paper money.

The Duke, on seeing what good had resulted from the issue of paper money, converted Law's bank to a royal establishment and had it put out another large amount of paper currency. This also proved initially beneficial. On the theory that if an issue of 500 million livres was good more issues of the same amount must be even better, the bank flooded the country with paper money on the Duke's orders. As usual, such excessive creation of money led to a virulent inflation. It also provided the wherewithal for the people of France to speculate in the stock of the Mississippi Company.

Grateful for his advice, the Duke had granted to Law the right to form a company that was to have the exclusive right of trading to the lands drained by the Mississippi River, an area believed to be full of gold and silver. The company was formed in August 1717, with shares issued for 500 livres each.

At the beginning of 1719, the Mississippi Company was granted another royal plum, the exclusive privilege of trading in the East Indies, China, and the South Seas. An offering of new shares was announced, and the public became so enthusiastic about the company that the offering was greatly oversubscribed. The public had excessive funds, because of the large amounts of paper currency that had been created. The street on which Law's house was located became the scene of frenzied trading in the stock of the Mississippi Company. The aristocracy as well as the lower classes had visions of boundless wealth.

Such was the volume of trading that houses on Law's street rented for amounts twelve to sixteen times above normal. A cobbler who had a stall was renting it out to brokers for a small fortune each day. A hunchbacked man who stood in the street gained substantial sums by lending his hump as a writing desk.

Everyone in Paris was preoccupied with the price movements of Mississippi Company stock. Mackay describes the preoccupation of a French doctor:

> M. de Chirac, a celebrated physician, had bought stock at an unlucky period, and was very anxious to sell out. Stock, however, continued to fall for two or three days, much to his alarm. His mind was filled with the subject, when he was suddenly called upon to attend a lady who imagined herself unwell. He arrived, was shewn up stairs, and felt the lady's pulse. "It falls! it falls! good God! it falls continually!" said he musingly, while the lady

looked up in his face all anxiety for his opinion. "Oh, M. de Chirac," said she, starting to her feet and ringing the bell for assistance; "I am dying! I am dying! it falls! it falls! it falls!" "What falls?" inquired the doctor in amazement. "My pulse! my pulse!" said the lady; "I must be dying." "Calm your apprehensions, my dear madam," said M. de Chirac; "I was speaking of the stocks. The truth is, I have been a great loser, and my mind is so disturbed, I hardly know what I have been saying."

The economy of Paris boomed as people flocked to the capital to trade in Mississippi Company stock. Luxury homes were built at a dizzying rate. Laces and velvets were in short supply and commanded premium prices. Pictures and statues were imported from foreign countries at an increasing rate.

The more acute observers realized that the party could not go on forever and began selling Mississippi stock and converting paper money into gold, silver, and jewelry, which they shipped to England and Holland. By February 1720, low limits were placed on the amount of gold coin that an individual could hold. This simply hastened the end.

Mississippi stock fell precipitately in price. In a last effort to support the stock, the government conscripted six thousand of Paris's poor and outfitted them with clothes and tools. They were paraded for several days through Paris, while the government circulated the story that they were going to work the enormous gold mines that existed in Louisiana and the Mississippi River territory. The charade had little effect. By the end of 1720, Law had fled the country, and Mississippi Company stock had become virtually worthless.

The second story that Baruch found of value in Mackay's book was the story of the South Sea Bubble. The English proved to be as susceptible to greed as the French. In 1711, the South Sea Company had been formed to assume a part of England's national debt in return for an annual payment of 600,000 pounds and a monopoly in trading with lands bordering on the South Seas. The most important of these areas were Chile, Peru, and Mexico. The public at this time believed that these countries contained inexhaustible wealth. They believed that all that was necessary was to send manufactured goods from England and fabulous amounts of gold and silver would be received in return. Spain, of course, had no intention of allowing this trade, but this fact was overlooked in the euphoria of the moment.

Through various stratagems, the name of the South Sea Company was kept before the public, and the enthusiasm for its stock was maintained. Then, in 1720, the directors conceived of a plan for the company to assume England's entire national debt in return for an annual payment by the government to the company. This proposal focused favorable public attention on the company, and its shares rose from 130 to 330 by the time Parliament accepted the proposal. In the meantime, the directors and others interested in the company circulated stories about the fabulous riches of South America. This inflamed the greed of the public. The stock rose higher and higher. It reached 500, then 680. One rumor, which buoyed the stock, was that Spain had agreed to trade several fortresses on the coast of Peru in exchange for Gibraltar. These fortresses would greatly facilitate British trade with the area. Finally, by August 1720, the price of South Sea stock reached 1,000.

The public frenzy to become rich was not satisfied by the South Sea Company. Trading sprang up in numerous newly formed stock companies, which were soon nicknamed "bubbles." Such was the public lust that companies were formed to carry out the most implausible schemes. Mackay describes three such companies:

> . . . One of them was for a wheel for perpetual motion—capital one million; another was "for encouraging the breed of horses in England, and improving of glebe and church lands, and repairing and rebuilding parsonage and vicarage houses." Why the clergy, who were so mainly interested in the latter clause, should have taken so much interest in the first, is only to be explained on the supposition that the scheme was projected by a knot of the fox-hunting parsons, once so common in England. The shares of this company were rapidly subscribed for. But the most absurd and preposterous of all, and which shewed, more completely than any other, the utter madness of the people, was one started by an unknown adventurer, entitled, "A company for carrying on an undertaking of great advantage, but nobody to know what it is."

While South Sea stock was soaring toward 1,000, Sir John Blunt, chairman of the company, and other astute individuals were unloading their stock. Ultimately, the weight of their selling and a more sober assessment of the prospects of the South Sea Company produced a crash in the price of the stock. By October, the price had fallen all the way to 135. Numerous bankruptcies followed.

A Parliamentary investigation ultimately disclosed that stock had been illegally issued to insiders and to influential politicians in order to gain their support. These individuals were compelled to pay substantial fines. Parliament also passed the Bubble Act in the hope of preventing a recurrence of the South Sea episode. In Parliament's words, it was: "An Act to Restrain the Extravagant and Unwarrantable Practice of Raising Money by Voluntary Subscriptions for Carrying on Projects Dangerous to the Trade and Subjects of the Kingdom." Human nature, however, cannot be changed by legislation, and in 1845, the Bubble Act notwithstanding, the Great Railway Mania engulfed England much as had the South Sea Bubble a hundred years earlier.

It is easy to laugh at the folly of people in earlier times. But financial manias are not limited to the past. They are a recurrent phenomenon. The mechanism of the Bandwagon Effect remains the same. Only the object of the mania changes.

The gold frenzy of 1979–80 provides a recent example. As inflation intensified in the Sixties and Seventies, many articles and books were written about precious metals as a hedge against inflation. Precious metals began to be seen by some investors as a good investment. By 1975, when it became legal for Americans to again own gold, bullion had reached $200 per ounce. With the opening of the vast United States market, it was thought that the American public would snap up large quantities of gold and drive its price up even further. However, the opposite occurred. The American public exhibited no frenzy to buy gold, and prices dropped steadily until gold reached $104 in August 1976.

At that point, most investors would not touch gold. Even many of gold's long-time boosters, the so-called "gold bugs," had lost faith. However, with a resurgence of inflation and a growing lack of confidence in the Carter Administration, gold's price began gradually climbing. As its price rose, more and more individuals were attracted to it. Coin shops frequently had long lines. Krugerrand sales were setting new records. Suddenly, the gold price was being quoted on the evening news along with the Dow Jones Industrial Average. It had reached the critical mass necessary to ignite the Bandwagon Effect. People who had given no consideration to buying gold at $104, in 1976, were suddenly clamoring to buy it at $600 and $700 in 1979. Buying gold had become the thing to do. It was thought to be a sure way to make money. Ultimately, as in all financial manias, the gold frenzy reached an unsustainable peak in January 1980, at $875. Since then, gold has had a dramatic setback all the way to $400.

This discussion is not intended to reflect on the investment merits of gold, but merely to show that we Americans are just as susceptible to financial mania as were the French and English of earlier times or our grandfathers in the 1920s. Human nature does not change. The chain-letter schemes operating as "pyramid parties" and "money games" which swept the country in recent years are another example of how difficult it is to resist the lure of apparently easy money.

The basic mechanism behind the Bandwagon Effect is that once a certain level is reached, rising prices generate their own enthusiasm. People who would not buy an investment at a low price will buy that same asset later if it has risen substantially in price. When people hear at a party how much money one of their friends has made in a particular investment, they begin to think, "I'm as smart as John. If he can make money in that investment, so can I." A rising price trend also quite naturally increases the confidence of the purchaser, since there is a strong tendency to assume that a trend will continue, particularly if there is a plausible story behind the investment. When these factors coalesce, the price rise can be dramatic—especially when a large part of the population remains to be attracted. Ultimately, however, prices are driven to unsustainable levels, and the price falls precipitately.

Sometime in the 1980s, the stock market will begin to be carried along by the Bandwagon Effect. The rise in underlying value generated by the R-Factor and inflation makes a sizable advance in stock prices inevitable at some point. People will begin to make money in stocks, and they will talk about it. Stockbrokers will no longer be pariahs at cocktail parties. Enthusiasm for stocks will build. New investors will be attracted, and the Bandwagon Effect will begin to operate. Once it is in full swing, there is no telling how high the market may go. Dow 3,000 may be too low.

KEY POINTS

1.‖ The Bandwagon Effect is our name for the tendency of people to follow a trend once it gains a certain momentum.

2.‖ History has shown that once the price of a tradable asset such as common stock or gold reaches a certain point, people tend to get carried away, and the price of the asset is taken to unsustainable levels. Rising prices generate their own enthusiasm.

3.‖ We believe that at some point in the Eighties stock prices will reach a level that will activate the Bandwagon Effect, and prices will be carried to extraordinary levels—perhaps well above 3,000.

CHAPTER 12
DOW
260,890,000,000,000

‖T WAS A stock market that not even King Midas, in his wildest dreams, could have imagined. The first year, prices gradually rose from 97 to 127. By the end of the second year, they were at 274. The following year, they were at 731. By the end of the fourth year, they were at 898. Trading on the stock exchange reached such a frenzy that the market was open only three days a week. It took the other days to catch up on the paperwork.

Everyone was involved in the market. A financial newspaper noted: "Today there is no one—from lift-boy, typist, and small landlord to the wealthy lady in high society—who does not speculate in industrial securities and who does not study the list of official quotations as if it were a most precious letter." Even the rural areas were infected. Telephone lines which connected these areas to the central city were jammed at certain times of the day as farmers inquired about stock prices and placed their orders.

By the fifth year, prices exploded and reached the extraordinary level of 260,890,000,000,000. That is not a misprint. The number is 260,890 followed by nine zeros. Stockbrokers had only good news for their clients. Stock prices had gone to the stratosphere. Imagine buying a stock at 100 and seeing its price reach 260,890,000,000,000. And that was just an average stock. Individual issues had even more spectacular rises. This description is not an imaginary one. It describes what actually occurred in Germany in the period 1919–23.

This period spawned one of the classic stories about the stock market. In its current version, the story goes like this:

Bill, a successful investor, goes into a coma after being struck by an automobile. At the time of the accident, Bill has a portfolio of stocks worth $50,000. After being in the coma for twenty years, Bill wakes up in the hospital. He immediately rushes to the pay phone in the hall and calls his broker.

Bill gets the broker on the line and says:

"John, this is Bill Smith. I recovered from the coma. What's my portfolio worth?"

The broker replies:

"It's great to hear from you, Bill. It's truly a miracle you survived the accident. Have I got good news for you! Your portfolio is now worth one million dollars."

While Bill is savoring this news, the telephone operator breaks in, saying:

"That will be fifty thousand dollars for the next three minutes."

The point of the story is that while Bill's stocks were going up, so were the prices of everything else. The apparent monetary gain was illusory.

This is precisely what occurred in Germany in 1919–23. Stock prices rose astronomically. But so did consumer prices. At one point, it took a wheelbarrow full of paper money to pay for a loaf of bread. Prices were rising so fast that the price of a meal in a restaurant could triple from the time a person ordered to the time he paid the bill.

The net effect of rising consumer prices in Germany was that from the beginning of 1919 until the end of 1923, the holder of common stocks actually lost 41 percent of his purchasing power, in spite of the astronomical rise in the stock market. This fact is cited by some observers to establish the fact that stocks are not a hedge against an inflation or a hyperinflation (an inflation in which prices rise hundreds of percent per year).

The problem with this conclusion is that it depends upon using the beginning of 1919 as the starting period for measurement. If the beginning of 1920 is used, the result is entirely different. From that time until the end of 1923, the investor would have actually gained purchasing power.

Chart G shows the behavior of German stocks, in terms of purchasing power, during this period. Notice the large drops in

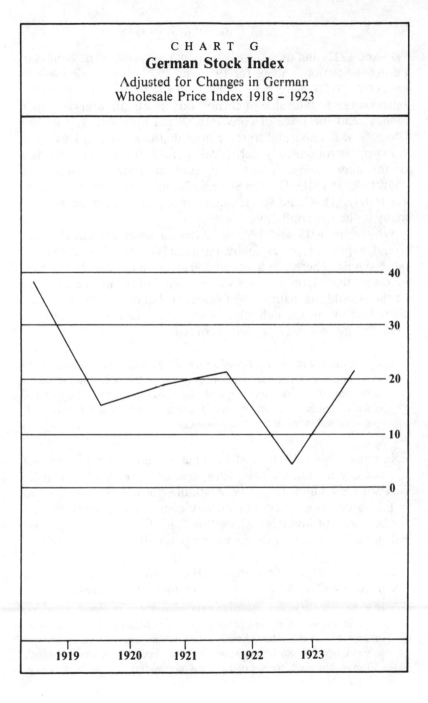

CHART G
German Stock Index
Adjusted for Changes in German
Wholesale Price Index 1918 – 1923

40

30

20

10

0

1919   1920   1921   1922   1923

1919 and 1922, and then the subsequent recoveries. The behavior during the period, except for 1919 and 1922, is what one would expect if stocks were being valued on the basis of their assets. Inflation raised the value of corporation assets, in terms of paper money, and the price of corporate shares followed. In viewing Chart G, it is important to remember that consumer prices were going up astronomically during this period. If they were plotted on the same scale as Chart G, it would be necessary to have a chart taller than the Empire State Building to show their behavior accurately. That's how much consumer prices went up in Germany in the hyperinflation.

Why were 1919 and 1922 so different from the pattern one would expect of prices following asset values? The answer is quite simple. There was a tremendous fear on the part of German investors that Germany, as a society, would not survive and that neither would the institution of private property. Professor Bresciani-Turroni, in the definitive work on the German hyperinflation, *The Economics of Inflation,* noted:

> Obviously the sharp fall of share prices which occurred in 1919 was in a very large part the consequence of the political and social disorganization of Germany, of the economic crisis, and of the lack of confidence which spread among the people when the advent of Bolshevism seemed imminent.

In evaluating 1919, it must be remembered that the Armistice did not occur until October 1918, and the Treaty of Versailles was not signed until July 1919. Also, the Russian Revolution was in full force. These factors naturally caused great consternation in the minds of investors. Once this fear of social disintegration had subsided, German stocks were again influenced by asset values.

A similar lack of confidence in the future of German society occurred in 1922. As Professor Bresciani-Turroni noted:

> . . . In the summer this feeling was accentuated by the consternation about the internal political situation, aggravated by the assassination of Rathenau, and by the reparations crisis, which France, the Conference of London having finished without result,

now threatened to determine by arms. It is certain that a great lack
of confidence spread among the German people in the summer of
1922.

This crisis of confidence passed, and by the end of 1923, German investors no longer feared for the survival of German society
or the institution of private property.

In 1924, after the German hyperinflation had been ended by
the introduction of a new currency, German companies were
required to prepare new balance sheets showing the value of their
assets and liabilities in terms of gold. The balance sheets could
then be compared with their pre–World War I balance sheets to
see what harm they had suffered through those tempestuous
eleven years.

The amazing fact is that the major German companies emerged
essentially intact from this turbulent era. As Professor Bresciani-
Turroni stated:

> . . . Generally the great companies of the mining and iron and
> steel industry, and the electrical and chemical industries, have
> preserved or increased their capital, compared with 1913. It is true
> that this was often due to the growth of firms after 1913, owing to
> the absorption of smaller firms, and to the reduction of mortgages,
> debentures, etc. However, *the fact is always important because it
> proves that the great German companies were able to resist the
> tempest loosed by the war, the defeat, the revolution and the
> inflation.* Examples of important companies which had been
> forced to reduce greatly their pre-war capital are not frequent.
> [Emphasis added.]

There you have it. The big companies survived. This really
should not be that surprising. After all, they had the most resources at their disposal in the fight for survival.

What caused the dramatic German hyperinflation? The answer
is excessive creation of money by the German government. It is
as simple as that. As Professor Bresciani-Turroni concluded:

> It was only the continual increase in the issues of legal money
> which made possible the incessant rise in prices and the continual
> fall in the external value of the mark, as has been demonstrated in
> the course of this book.

Why did the German government create so much money? The government created the money to fund its budget deficit. Throughout World War I, Germany refused to raise taxes to a level sufficient to balance its budget. This policy was continued through the early Twenties, with tragic results. Table VI gives the actual figures of the German budget expressed in terms of gold to eliminate the distorting effect of the change in the value of the mark.

TABLE VI

Income and Expenditures of the German Government, 1919–1923 (in Millions of Gold Marks)

	INCOME	EXPENDITURE
1919	2,559	8,559
1920	3,178	9,328
1921	2,927	6,651
1922	1,488	3,950
1923	518	5,278

Anyone who doubts the wisdom or necessity of achieving a balanced United States federal budget in the coming years should consider the German experience.

KEY POINTS

1.‖The behavior of stock prices during the German hyperinflation supports our thesis that liquidating values have a great influence on stock prices.
2.‖The German hyperinflation was caused by excessive creation of money by the German government. That government created excessive amounts of money to finance its massive budget deficits.
3.‖The German experience emphasizes how important it is that the United States government balance the federal budget as quickly as possible.

CHAPTER 13
IT WENT WRONG

ONE OF OUR friends is a very dynamic Chinese entrepreneur. One of his favorite expressions when something goes awry is, "It went wrong." Our friend recently told us the story of Seven Samurai, which we found to be particularly appropriate for this chapter.

It seems that a man on his seventy-seventh birthday went to the greyhound races to bet on a specific dog. The man was a seventh son of a seventh son, and he had a very strong feeling about a dog running in the seventh race named Seven Samurai. His strong feelings had frequently been right in the past, and he had made substantial sums at the greyhound races. Seven Samurai was in the seventh post position and showed odds of seven to one. The man, feeling he had a sure thing, bet $777 to win on Seven Samurai. After a fast start, Seven Samurai ended up finishing . . . seventh. As our friend would say, "It went wrong."

While we believe that circumstances strongly favor the Dow's reaching 3,000 by 1989, there are most certainly things that can go wrong with this forecast. Obviously, a nuclear war would negate it. So also would the nationalization of the Dow companies. However, while these threats are real, we assign a low probability to their occurrence.

A more likely problem would be a severe energy crisis. If OPEC suddenly shut off the flow of oil, the consequences could be devastating. It would be very difficult for the United States economy to adapt. Our society would survive, but only at a much reduced economic level. This reduced economic level would be reflected in lower stock prices.

A more gradual reduction of oil supplies would not necessarily upset our forecast. American industry has shown great adaptability with respect to energy usage. Each year since 1974, industry has been able to increase the output generated per unit of energy input. The aluminum industry, for example, is now producing at least 10 percent more aluminum per unit of energy than it did in 1974.

The current energy crisis, in certain respects, will probably be beneficial to America in that it creates a challenge. From an economic standpoint, challenges have been beneficial as they stimulate new inventions and new techniques. Wars, the most extreme form of challenge, have led to technical developments of enormous economic benefit to later generations. It is likely that the energy crisis will result in new developments in geothermal power, solar technology, fusion power, synthetic fuels, genetic engineering, and a host of other technologies.

Similarly, the economic challenge from Japan, while having a very negative impact on certain sectors of our economy, should also be beneficial in the long run. It is forcing American companies to improve the quality of their products to match the high Japanese standards. It is also leading to a revolution in management in which greater emphasis will be placed on involving workers in the production process. American employees in United States plants operated by Japanese companies such as Sony are proving to be as productive as Japanese workers. The difference between the United States and Japan apparently is not in the quality of the workers, but in management techniques.

Another possible event that could alter our forecast would be a major depression. Several individuals have prophesied just such a depression for the Eighties. While a depression is possible, we believe that it has a low probability of occurring. The reason we think this is the fact that the government now plays such a major role in the economy. Should a major depression begin developing, the government is likely to take whatever measures are necessary to prevent it. The measures might entail massive inflation, but, politically, inflation is a lesser evil than depression and widespread unemployment.

While the economic record in recent years has clearly shown that it is impossible to "fine-tune" the economy, the government does have the weapons at its disposal to counteract a depression. The most likely countermeasures would be massive deficit spending and a substantial expansion of the money supply—measures that were not taken at the onset of the Great Depression. Rather, as Milton Friedman, Nobel Prize winner in economics, notes in his book *Free to Choose,* the Great Depression was intensified and prolonged by the fact that the Federal Reserve allowed a one-third reduction in the domestic money supply. It is unlikely that such a mistake will be made in the future.

As we indicated in Chapter 1, the stock market seldom goes straight up. The great bull markets of the Twenties and Fifties were both interrupted by sharp declines. We would not consider a substantial drop in the Dow in the next few years as negating our forecast of Dow 3,000, unless it is caused by a change in the underlying mechanisms determining long-term stock prices. If, for example, the decline is caused by a sharp increase in the capital gains tax or some type of punitive corporate tax, then the forecast would probably have to be abandoned. If, however, the decline is caused by anticipation of a sub-par economy for the next year, we would not be concerned. In that event, we would simply view the decline as offering another opportunity to buy stocks at very favorable prices. Great bull markets frequently offer investors a second and third chance to get aboard before they really explode upward.

Unless there is a change in the underlying mechanisms, the longer stock prices remain depressed, the more dramatic will be the ultimate advance. The buildup of corporate values is like the injection of steam into a boiler with no safety valve. The process can go on for a long time with no apparent change, but at some point the pressure becomes so great that the boiler explodes. We believe that we are rapidly approaching an explosion in the American stock market.

KEY POINTS

1.‖ Our forecast of Dow 3,000 can be upset by, among other things, a nuclear war, nationalization of the Dow companies, a depression, or a complete shut-off of OPEC oil. While these occurrences are possible, we don't believe that they will occur in the Eighties.

2.‖ We would not consider a substantial decline in the Dow as negating our forecast of Dow 3,000, unless it is caused by a change in the fundamental mechanisms generating long-term stock prices. A large increase in the capital gains tax rate or the adoption of much higher corporate taxes would be two of the factors that would cause us to revise our forecast.

3.‖ Great bull markets frequently offer investors a second or third chance to buy stocks at very favorable prices. If the Dow should drop in anticipation of a temporary decline in corporate profits or the economy, we would view such a decline as an extraordinary opportunity to establish long-term stock positions at very, very favorable prices.

The Specific Forecasts

PART II

CHAPTER 1
THE METHOD

HAVE YOU NOTICED that as you grow older time seems to pass faster?

One year now seems to pass much faster than a year did when you were five years old. When you were in the first or second grade, a year was an eternity. A year now seems to zip by. Perhaps you have relatives in their seventies or eighties. People this age frequently remark how ten years seem to pass as quickly as a year.

Why is this so?

The explanation for this phenomenon is that we judge time in relation to our previous experience. A five-year-old has only had five years of experience. One year is one-fifth or 20 percent of his life. A fifty-year-old has had fifty years of experience. One year is only one-fiftieth or 2 percent of his life. Since each passing year represents a smaller and smaller fraction of our total experience, each year subjectively seems to pass faster and faster. That's why time seems to fly as we grow older.

What is true of our judgment of time is also true of our judgment of the stock market. There is a very powerful tendency to view the stock market in relation to our previous experience. For the past fifteen years, most investors in the stocks on which the Dow Jones Industrial Average is based have not had a rewarding experience. There is a quite natural tendency to expect the condition to continue. This expectation, however, is unlikely to prove correct. As we have seen, there are very powerful forces that should drive the Dow to 3,000 and above. Investors in the coming fifteen years should have a very profitable experience.

The exact nature of an investor's experience with the Dow

stocks will depend on precisely which of the thirty he owns and how those particular stocks perform. In the Fifties, when the Dow tripled in a decade, not all of the Dow stocks rose by the same amount. Some rose only 50 percent. Others rose 1,000 percent. The Dow, after all, is an average. And an average can conceal very divergent moves in its individual components.

In this part of the book, we are going to explore the possible price appreciation of each of the current thirty Dow stocks. We will discuss them in the order that they actually performed in the Fifties. We project that some of the Dow stocks are going to have spectacular rises in the Eighties. For others, we project only mediocre gains. One company, we project, will be dropped from the Dow.

It should be emphasized that we are much more confident that our forecast of a Dow of 3,000 will be realized than we are that our forecast for any particular Dow stock will be realized. The reason is that a great many circumstances peculiar to a company or its industry can upset the forecast for an individual stock. In an aggregate such as the Dow, however, these influences tend to cancel each other out.

It should also be emphasized that we are limiting our discussion to just the thirty companies in the Dow Jones Industrial Average. There are well over four thousand other companies with common stock readily available in the United States. It is highly probable that many of these other stocks will outperform even the best performers in the Dow. Thus the investor should not stop at the thirty Dow stocks in investigating candidates for his portfolio.

With these caveats in mind, let's now proceed to the actual method that we have used to forecast the price of each of the thirty Dow stocks in 1989. In Chapter 6 of Part I, we used the following formula to project a price for the Dow in 1989:

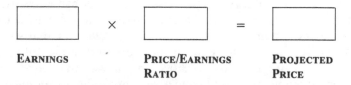

| EARNINGS | × | PRICE/EARNINGS RATIO | = | PROJECTED PRICE |

This same formula can be used to project a price for each of the thirty Dow stocks. To apply the formula, it is necessary to generate an estimate of each company's 1989 earnings per share and the Price/Earnings Ratio that will apply to those earnings. Those readers who are not interested in the details of how our forecasts are derived might wish to skip the rest of the chapter.

THE EARNINGS ESTIMATE

In Chapter 2 of Part I, we discussed how a savings account would grow over time if only half of the interest was withdrawn each year. We produced the following table which traced exactly how the growth in the account occurred:

TABLE III

Savings Account at 10%, Half of Interest Withdrawn Each Year (Figures Rounded)

YEAR	BEGINNING BALANCE	INTEREST EARNED	INTEREST WITHDRAWN	ENDING BALANCE
1	$1,000	$100	$50	$1,050
2	1,050	105	53	1,103
3	1,103	110	55	1,158
4	1,158	116	58	1,216
5	1,216	122	61	1,277
6	1,277	128	64	1,341
7	1,341	(134)	67	1,407

Notice how once we knew the starting balance in the account ($1,000), the after-tax interest rate (10 percent), and the amount of interest withdrawn (½), it was possible to derive the amount in the account at the end of any particular year. More important, it was also possible to derive the total amount of interest that would be earned in any given year. For example, in year seven, the account would earn a total of $134 in interest. We have circled this number in the table. To repeat, once we know the starting balance, the after-tax interest rate, and the amount of interest retained, we can compute the interest earned on the account for any year in the future. All that is involved is simple arithmetic.

We can use this same procedure to derive what each Dow

company should earn in 1989. The corporate equivalent of the $1,000 starting balance in our hypothetical savings account is Beginning Book Value per Share. This is simply the Book Value that we have previously discussed expressed on a per-share basis: Total Book Value/Common Shares Outstanding = Book Value per Share. Remember, Book Value is calculated according to the formula Assets − Liabilities* = Book Value. It is a measure of the amount of money invested in the company.

The corporate equivalent of the 10 percent after-tax interest rate earned on our hypothetical savings account is called the Return on Book Value. This is the rate of return that the company is earning on the money invested in the company. For example, if a company had a Book Value of $100 per share at the beginning of the year, and it earned $20 in profits during the year, its Return on Book Value would be $20/$100 = 20 percent.

The corporate equivalent of the half of the interest withdrawn in our hypothetical savings account is called the Payout Ratio. This is the percent of earnings that the company pays out in dividends. For example, if a company earned $20 in profits in a year and paid out $10 in dividends, its Payout Ratio would be $10/$20 = 50 percent.

It may be helpful to review so that our terminology is clearly understood:

Savings Account	Corporate Equivalent
Beginning balance	= Beginning Book Value per Share
Ending balance	= Ending Book Value per Share
After-tax interest rate	= Return on Book Value
Part of interest withdrawn	= Payout Ratio
Interest earned	= Earnings per Share
Interest withdrawn	= Dividends per Share

Table VII demonstrates how we used these concepts to estimate Procter & Gamble's earnings in 1989. Underneath the headings we have placed, in parentheses, the equivalent headings from the savings account example.

* Includes the liquidating value of any preferred shares.

TABLE VII

	Beginning Book Value		=	$43.52
	Assumed Return on			
	Book Value		=	16.5%
	Assumed Payout Ratio		=	45.0%

YEAR	BEGINNING BOOK VALUE (BEGINNING BALANCE)	EARNINGS (INTEREST EARNED)	DIVIDENDS (INTEREST WITHDRAWN)	ENDING BOOK VALUE (ENDING BALANCE)
1981	43.52	7.18	3.23	47.47
1982	47.47	7.83	3.52	51.78
1983	51.78	8.54	3.84	56.48
1984	56.48	9.32	4.19	61.61
1985	61.61	10.17	4.57	67.21
1986	67.21	11.09	4.99	73.31
1987	73.31	12.10	5.44	79.97
1988	79.97	13.20	5.94	87.23
1989	87.23	(14.39)	6.48	95.14

Based upon its 1980 balance sheet, Procter & Gamble had a Book Value per Share of $43.52. We have assumed that Procter & Gamble will earn 16.5 percent on Book Value and that it will pay out 45 percent of its earnings in the form of dividends.

Multiplying the Beginning Book Value per Share ($43.52) times the Assumed Return on Book Value (.165) gives us estimated earnings of $7.18 in 1981. Multiplying these earnings of $7.18 by the Payout Ratio (.45) gives us an estimated dividend of $3.23. If we subtract the dividends from the earnings, we arrive at $3.95. This is the amount that is being reinvested in the company (the R-Factor). We add this sum to the Beginning Book Value to arrive at the Ending Book Value for the year. The Ending Book Value becomes the next year's Beginning Book Value, and the process is repeated.

Table VII shows how these projections work out through 1989. We have circled the earnings figure of $14.39 in 1989, since this is the number that we will be entering into the earnings box in our valuation formula.

Notice that to make our earnings projection for Procter &

Gamble we had to make only two assumptions—one for Return on Book Value and one for the Payout Ratio. We didn't have to make an assumption for the Beginning Book Value, since the actual number was derived from Procter & Gamble's balance sheet. Over time, the Payout Ratio for most companies tends to be fairly constant. The Return on Book Value, however, tends to be much less stable. If our earnings projections err, it will most probably be because we erred in estimating the Return on Book Value.

It should be noted that our estimates for Return on Book Value are an average for the entire nine-year period, 1981–89. In sub-par business years, we would anticipate that the actual Return on Book Value would be less than our nine-year-average estimate, and, in above-par business years, it would be above our nine-year-average estimate. Overall, however, the actual Return on Book Value should approximate our nine-year-average estimate or our 1989 earnings projections will be off, possibly substantially.

THE PRICE/EARNINGS RATIO
ESTIMATE

In our valuation formula for Procter & Gamble, we have entered the estimated 1989 earnings of 14.39 in the appropriate box.

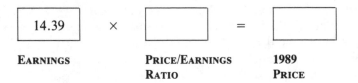

| 14.39 | × | | = | |
| EARNINGS | | PRICE/EARNINGS RATIO | | 1989 PRICE |

The question now is: What Price/Earnings Ratio do we put in the other box?

Rather than arbitrarily pick Price/Earnings Ratios out of the air, we have made the assumption that by 1989 each Dow company will have a Price/Earnings Ratio equal to halfway between the high and the low Price/Earnings Ratio that actually prevailed for the company in the period 1971–80. For example, Procter &

Gamble had a high Price/Earnings Ratio of 33 and a low Price/
Earnings Ratio of 8 during this period. Halfway between these
numbers is 20.5 (33 ⌐ 8 divided by 2). Thus, we have entered the
figure 20.5 in the Price/Earnings Ratio box:

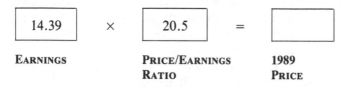

EARNINGS   PRICE/EARNINGS   1989
                    RATIO   PRICE

Notice that we are only taking the *midpoint* of the range in the
Price/Earnings Ratios that *actually prevailed* for each company
in the period 1971–80. We could have taken the highest Price/
Earnings Ratio attained in the decade and achieved much higher
projected prices, but we wanted to allow a substantial margin for
contingencies.

The Price/Earnings Ratio can be viewed as a measure of the
confidence that investors have in the future of a company. In
essence, the assumption underlying our use of average Price/
Earnings Ratios is that investor confidence during the Eighties
will return to an average level. In the early Seventies, investors
were optimistic about the outlook for many companies, and their
Price/Earnings Ratios were generally high. In the late Seventies,
investors became pessimistic about most companies, and their
Price/Earnings Ratios have been low. By the end of the Eighties,
we believe that confidence will have returned to at least an average level.

Multiplying out the numbers in the formula for Procter & Gamble results in a projected 1989 price of $295. This compares with
its September 8, 1981, price of $68.

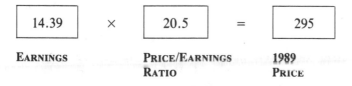

EARNINGS   PRICE/EARNINGS   1989
                    RATIO   PRICE

We have used exactly the same procedure to project the 1989
price of each of the Dow stocks. For each stock, we show the

Assumed Payout Ratio, the Assumed Return on Book Value, and the Assumed Price/Earnings Ratio, as well as the actual historical numbers for the period 1971–80. We have done this so that you or your stockbroker or investment adviser can evaluate the reasonableness of our assumptions. If you wish, you can calculate your own 1989 prices based upon your own assumptions using the format we have set forth in this chapter. A worksheet for this purpose is placed at the end of this chapter.

Two technical points should be noted. To be consistent, the Book Value that we have used for each company is the Book Value that Dow Jones and Company used in computing the overall Book Value of the Dow Jones Industrial Average. These Book Values are adjusted for intangible items and other factors and are not always the same numbers that the individual companies have reported in their annual reports. Also, in computing Return on Book Value, we have divided the current year's earnings by the prior year's Book Value.

If our projections of individual 1989 stock prices are combined, the result is a Dow Jones Industrial Average of 3,081 (adjusting for stock splits that have occurred since December 31, 1980). If our projections of individual company earnings are combined, the result is $225. Dividing price by earnings, we find that the Price/Earnings Ratio is 13.2. These results are entirely consistent with those determined in Chapter 6 of Part I, where we valued the Dow based on aggregate numbers.

INFLATION-ADJUSTED BOOK VALUE

We have not attempted to value each company by projecting an inflation-adjusted Book Value. The reason is that in the case of any particular company, these values can be very misleading. Unlike reported Earnings per Share, which are based on actual transactions, companies of necessity have to make many, many estimates of current plant costs, machinery prices, etc., in computing inflation-adjusted Book Value. The accuracy of these estimates can vary widely from company to company. In their annual reports, many companies warn of the experimental nature of these numbers and of the danger in using them literally. We have felt justified in using them for the Dow Jones Industrial Average as a whole only because we believe that when they are aggregated, the variations from company to company tend to offset each other. Again, this is the principle that an aggregate number tends to be more reliable than any individual component.

‖ WORKSHEET

Stock:_____

Assumed Return on Book:_____

Assumed Payout Ratio:_____

Assumed Price/Earnings Ratio:_____

Year	Beginning Book Value	Earnings	Dividend	Ending Book Value

$$\boxed{} \times \boxed{} = \boxed{}$$

Earnings   **Assumed P/E**   **Forecast Price**

CHAPTER 2
GOODYEAR

RETURN ON BOOK VALUE	PAYOUT RATIO	PRICE/EARNINGS RATIO
71–80 High: 13.2%	71–80 High: 65%	71–80 High: 15
71–80 Low: 6.7%	71–80 Low: 33%	71–80 Low: 4
Assumed: 10.0%	Assumed: 40%	Assumed: 9.5

1981 Beginning Book Value per Share: $32.09

WE ARE DISCUSSING Goodyear first because Goodyear had the largest percentage price increase of any Dow stock in the Fifties. The other companies will be discussed in the order in which they performed in that decade.

Goodyear is unlikely to repeat its spectacular performance of the 1950s. Economic trends that ran in its favor in the Fifties are now moving in the opposite direction. Goodyear, however, is responding to the problems that beset the tire industry in the way that a corporation should respond to a fundamental problem. It is adopting a long-range strategy to deal with the problem and rejecting the temptation to make only cosmetic changes.

As we have mentioned, Wall Street tends to focus on the short term—what a company will earn next quarter or next year. This myopia puts tremendous pressure on corporate executives to produce results in the short term. The effect is that many executives understandably succumb to the pressure and resort to the "quick fix." By using a variety of tricks, executives can boost short-term earnings. These actions, however, do nothing to solve the fundamental problems facing a corporation and, if long continued, can destroy its competitive position. Fortunately, Goodyear's management has not succumbed to this temptation.

Considering the name of the company, it would seem to be a reasonable assumption that a man named Goodyear founded it. After all, a du Pont founded Du Pont, a Sears founded Sears, and a Procter and Gamble founded Procter & Gamble. Nonetheless, Goodyear was started by a man named Frank Silberling. Silberling named the company Goodyear to honor Charles Goodyear, the man who invented vulcanization—the process that made the tire industry possible.

Charles Goodyear was known as the "India rubber maniac." His fascination with rubber began in 1834, while he was searching for a way to pay off the heavy debts that he owed as a result of a failed hardware business. As he glanced in a store window one day, he observed an inflated rubber life preserver with a rather primitive inflating valve. While he was discussing the valve with the store manager, the manager suggested that the way to make a lot of money would be to come up with a process that would prevent rubber from melting in summer and freezing and sticking in winter. These problems had aborted a rubber boom that had started in the United States in 1830.

In 1830, the problems with rubber were quite clear to Daniel Webster, the famous orator and lawyer. He had purchased one of the newly produced India rubber coats and hats only to find that when he stepped outside one day into a sub-zero temperature, his coat froze solid and stuck to the front porch. Easing out of the coat, he placed the frozen hat on top of the frozen coat, which stood rigidly erect. Thinking Webster was on the porch, friends waved greetings to the stiff figure.

Anticipating the financial rewards that would result from solving the problems of rubber, Goodyear optimistically began experimenting. Many of these early experiments were carried out in jail, since Goodyear had not been able to pay off his debts. After several years of frustration, Goodyear met a man who had had some success dissolving sulfur into rubber. While arguing with friends one day, Goodyear accidentally dropped a glob of the rubber-sulfur mixture onto a red-hot kitchen stove. Surprisingly, the mixture did not melt and was not sticky. Further improvements led to the vulcanization process.

Even though he had made rubber commercially attractive, Goodyear did not reap huge profits. In order to meet his debts, he was forced to sell licenses for his process very cheaply. He continued, however, to be obsessed with rubber. By the time of his death, in 1860, Goodyear had some sixty patents listing nearly five hundred uses for rubber.

Amazingly, in all of the uses for rubber that he thought up, Goodyear overlooked what was to become the most important —the tire. Frank Silberling, however, did not. Borrowing $1,500, he founded the Goodyear Tire and Rubber Company in an abandoned factory in East Akron, Ohio, in 1898. Although Goodyear's first products were bicycle tires, the company soon focused on supplying tires for the burgeoning automobile industry. Goodyear pioneered the development of tubeless, pneumatic, and sidewall tires.

By 1916, Goodyear had become the world's largest tire company, and Frank Silberling was known as the "Little Napoleon of Rubber." He was only five feet three inches tall and had a domineering personality. After World War I, the Little Napoleon met his Waterloo. He had contracted for a large supply of crude rubber at peak prices right before the postwar depression. The resulting losses forced the company into the hands of a group of bankers who replaced Silberling. Reorganized, Goodyear benefited from the enormous growth of the automobile industry.

Goodyear's best years occurred after World War II. With cheap gasoline, people drove farther in heavier, more luxurious cars. The expanding economy allowed people to buy second and third cars. These trends produced added tire sales, and Goodyear's profits dramatically increased. During the Fifties, its stock price rocketed up over 1,400 percent.

At the present, Goodyear, along with the rest of the tire industry, has fallen on hard times. Expensive gasoline has caused people to drive less and to purchase lighter cars. This means that their tires last longer. High interest rates, a sagging economy, and high car prices have dramatically cut new-car sales. Foreign competition, especially from the French tire maker Michelin, has put severe pressure on profit margins. The net effect of these factors has been to devastate America's tire manufacturers financially. 1980 was the worst year in history for the American tire industry. Goodyear, however, remained profitable on the strength of its foreign business.

In the face of these problems, Goodyear has adopted what appears to be the most rational strategy that it can follow, given the difficult prospects facing the tire industry. Rather than try for a "quick fix," Goodyear has adopted a long-term strategy of becoming the lowest-cost producer of the highest-quality tires. In order to achieve this goal, Goodyear has invested large sums in new automated plants. In the last few years, the company has also emphasized worker involvement, using many of the techniques that the Japanese pioneered.

Investing heavily in efficient plants in a slow-growth industry can be a recipe for low profits if the competition also invests in new plants. The reason Goodyear's strategy is likely to work is that its chief competitors appear unwilling or unable to match Goodyear's investment in new plants. Goodyear thus stands an excellent chance of becoming the lowest-cost producer in the tire industry.

Goodyear has resisted the lure of diversification. It has chosen to concentrate its resources to maintain and expand its dominant position in tires. Goodyear currently holds about one-third of the U.S. tire market. If it can successfully increase that market share, adequate profits should eventually follow. The key to an expanding market share will be offering high-quality products.

Based upon the method outlined in Chapter 1 of Part II, we project that Goodyear stock will rise in price from $18 to $49 a share by the end of the decade—an increase of 172 percent.

CHAPTER 3
MINNESOTA MINING & MANUFACTURING

RETURN ON BOOK VALUE	PAYOUT RATIO	PRICE/EARNINGS RATIO
71–80 High: 25.2%	71–80 High: 59%	71–80 High: 40
71–80 Low: 15.4%	71–80 Low: 40%	71–80 Low: 8
Assumed: 20.0%	Assumed: 50%	Assumed: 24

1981 Beginning Book Value per Share: $28.09

BASED UPON THE method outlined in Chapter 1 of Part II, we project that Minnesota Mining & Manufacturing stock will rise in price from $49 to $289 a share by the end of the decade—an increase of 490 percent.

3M is one of the relatively few giant American companies that is in a position to control its own destiny. Its enviable prospects are the result of its proven ability to create a continuous stream of profitable new products. 3M has been able to overcome the major problem that plagues most large corporations—lack of creativity. Most large corporations become so bureaucratized that their overwhelming concern is to play it safe. By and large, the executives that tend to be promoted are the ones that don't make mistakes and don't rock the boat. It is not surprising that creative, entrepreneurial individuals tend to leave such an environment, further reinforcing the conservative bias in the large corporation. 3M has resisted this tendency and has created a unique structure that rewards innovation and creativity. To a remarkable extent for a $6 billion enterprise, the company retains and develops the entrepreneurial individual, the person that creates the new businesses and new products that are essential to growth.

Minnesota Mining & Manufacturing owes its origin to a mistake. Around the turn of the century, a deposit of what was believed to be corundum was discovered in northern Minnesota near Lake Superior. Corundum is one of the hardest of minerals and is widely used in abrasives. An unlikely group of investors (a doctor, a lawyer, a butcher, and two railroad workers) each chipped in $1,000 to form a company with the grand title of Minnesota Mining & Manufacturing for the purpose of mining the supposed corundum deposit. After establishing a quarrying plant, the company was able to sell just one ton of the material in bulk for a total of $20, as it seemed to be worthless.

3M avoided bankruptcy only with the financial assistance of a St. Paul, Minnesota, plumbing executive. It stayed afloat manufacturing sandpaper, finally using conventional materials in place of its supposed corundum. Some years later, it was discovered that the "corundum" was really anorthosite, a low-grade mineral worthless as an abrasive.

In the Twenties, 3M developed "Wetordry," the first sandpaper that could be used with water. This product was an enormous success as it eliminated the dust hazard in the rapidly growing auto industry. 3M also developed masking tape, which solved, among other things, the problem of painting two-tone cars. Glues and adhesives on other tapes damaged a car's paint when they were removed.

Minnesota Mining & Manufacturing's most recognized product, Scotch brand cellophane tape, evolved out of an order received by a St. Paul firm to insulate several hundred railway refrigerator cars. The company turned to 3M for help when it found that the insulation would have to be wrapped and sealed to protect against moisture. While working on the problem, 3M's Richard Drew ran into another 3M researcher who was considering packaging 3M's masking tape with cellophane, a new product developed by Du Pont. Drew decided to coat the moisture-proof cellophane with adhesive and try it as a sealing tape for the insulation slabs. His idea didn't solve the refrigerator-car problem, but further experimenting resulted in the creation of Scotch tape.

3M's tradition of innovation and problem solving began with William McKnight, the guiding force behind the company for several decades. McKnight joined the company, in 1907, as an assistant bookkeeper, after he had been turned down the year before when he had applied for a job as a laborer. Upon becoming sales manager, McKnight, who had no formal sales experience, evolved a novel practice. Rather than call at the front office of a potential customer as salesmen traditionally did, McKnight would go to the production areas, where he would discuss with workers the things that they liked and disliked about the products they used in their work. Many useful product ideas came from these discussions, and 3M has continued the practice of actively soliciting customers' suggestions. Approximately 50 percent of 3M's new product ideas come from this source.

Listening to customers, however, is only one ingredient in the process of innovation at 3M. The structure of the company itself has been deliberately designed to foster new products. If a person at 3M has an idea for a potential product, he or she is encouraged to pursue the idea. Multiple sources of funding for new projects are available within the company. If the person with the idea can't persuade his or her own division to fund it, the person is free to seek funding from any of the company's other thirty-nine divisions or from special sources made available to new projects. Division managers are particularly anxious to assist anyone with a new product idea, since one of the key criteria that they are judged on is their ability to bring out successful new products. It is a corporate goal that 25 percent of each division's sales come from new products developed in the last five years. At 3M there is, in effect, a commandment: "Thou shall not kill a new idea."

Once the person has lined up funding for the project, he or she must recruit people to work on it. This has proved to be a valuable means of separating good product ideas from bad ones. If the person can't recruit people to work on his or her idea, chances are it isn't going to be a commercially successful product. Once the person has recruited his or her project team, the team is allowed to stay together, unless the project fails to meet certain simple, objective criteria. As long as the project meets the criteria, it is allowed to continue. If it grows to a sufficient size, it may become a separate division in itself.

One of the ways that 3M encourages people to take the risk of starting a new project is to assure them that, in effect, if they should fail at the project, they will be given a job equivalent to their old job somewhere in the company. This practice eliminates the financial penalties of failure that so often thwart budding entrepreneurs with family obligations.

It is a tribute to 3M's treatment of its employees that "headhunters" (executive recruiters) have an exceptionally difficult time luring managers away. The company was selected by *Money* magazine as one of the ten best companies to work for.

The success of the 3M approach can be measured by the enormous growth of the company. In 1940, the company had two divisions. Today, it has forty. Each division is operated essentially as a separate company. It finances new projects, builds factories, devises and implements marketing strategies, etc. New divisions are created as new product lines develop. 3M is really an aggregate of little companies rather than one big company.

In the 1970s, Minnesota Mining & Manufacturing's growth was temporarily interrupted by dislocations caused by the rise in oil prices and by wage and price guidelines set by the federal government. These problems have been overcome, and 3M is once again on a strong growth trend. In any one year earnings may dip slightly because of foreign currency problems (40 percent of 3M's sales come from foreign countries), but, overall, we expect Minnesota Mining & Manufacturing's continuous stream of new products to fuel an impressive rise in earnings and in its stock price in the Eighties.

CHAPTER 4
IBM

RETURN ON BOOK VALUE	PAYOUT RATIO	PRICE/EARNINGS RATIO
71–80 High: 24.9%	71–80 High: 67%	71–80 High: 39
71–80 Low: 18.1%	71–80 Low: 42%	71–80 Low: 8
Assumed: 20.0%	Assumed: 50%	Assumed: 23.5

1981 Beginning Book Value per Share: $28.49

ALL STREET IS preoccupied with the short term. It values most highly the company which can produce smooth predictable earnings increases regularly quarter after quarter. Few companies were more successful than IBM in the Fifties and Sixties in delivering what Wall Street wanted. As a consequence, IBM stock rose fabulously, and its name became synonymous with the term "growth stock."

In recent years, however, IBM's earnings have become more erratic, and its stock price has gone nowhere. In 1973, it sold as high as 91. In 1981, it has been as low as 53. Is IBM through as a growth stock?

We think not. In fact, we project IBM to be among the best performers of the Dow stocks in the 1980s. We believe that a rare opportunity has been created in IBM by the stock market's myopia. In the last several years, IBM has been laying the groundwork for explosive growth in the Eighties. This groundwork has been expensive and has penalized earnings. Wall Street has focused on the short-term earnings sluggishness and has ignored the enhanced future outlook. We believe that the stock market has unfairly penalized IBM for adopting a long-term strategy of growth. Once that growth becomes apparent, however, we anticipate that Wall Street will jump on the bandwagon, and IBM stock will once again soar.

Based upon the method outlined in Chapter 1 of Part II, we project that IBM stock will rise in price from $54 to $287 a share by the end of the decade—an increase of 431 percent.

When one thinks of IBM management, one immediately thinks of the name Watson. Thomas Watson, Sr., and Thomas Watson, Jr., guided the company for over fifty years, turning it into one of America's premier companies. However, the Watsons did not start IBM. It took a promoter named Charles Randall Flint to put together, in 1911, an amalgamation of companies that made meat slicers, cheese cutters, grocery scales, time clocks, and tabulating machines. He gave his amalgamation the impressive name of Computing-Tabulating-Recording Company.

Flint hired Thomas Watson, Sr., in 1914, to act as general manager of the firm. At the time, one of the directors objected to Flint's choice of Watson in the following words: "What are you trying to do, ruin the business? Who is going to run the business while he serves his term in jail?" It seems that Watson, while working for National Cash Register, had been convicted of a criminal conspiracy to restrain trade under the antitrust laws. Fortunately for IBM's stockholders (the company was renamed IBM in 1924), Watson's conviction was set aside on a technicality, and he was able to assume his new position without delay.

One of the consequences of Watson's close brush with jail was that he insisted that IBM scrupulously abide by all laws. It is ironic that IBM has had to spend the last twelve years and hundreds of millions of dollars defending itself against a government antitrust suit.

During Watson's first few years at Computing-Tabulating-Recording Company, increasing emphasis was put on the tabulating machine division. It had been formed to find commercial applications for the tabulating machine developed by Herman Hollerith for use in compiling statistics for the U.S. Census of 1890. Hollerith's invention was the forerunner of the punch-card machine.

In the Depression, Watson kept his production workers on full-time making tabulating machines and stored growing inventories of them in warehouses. The gamble paid off when Social Security and other New Deal programs were enacted. These programs required detailed accounting, which the stockpiled IBM machines could readily accomplish.

During World War II, IBM helped to organize the American war effort. The company developed new military uses for tabulating machines. Company historians have claimed that IBM machines helped break the Japanese code before the Battle of Midway and predicted the weather over the English Channel for the Normandy invasion.

Surprisingly, IBM did not develop the first electrical computer. This was accomplished by a team from the University of Pennsylvania. This team later developed the first commercial computer with a stored program, naming their creation UNIVAC. It was first offered to IBM for marketing, but Watson turned it down. Remington-Rand, IBM's chief competitor at the time, agreed to market it. Fortunately for IBM, Remington-Rand never committed the capital necessary to develop and distribute UNIVAC properly. Otherwise, it might have been the leading company in the computer age.

IBM also was offered the process for xerography about this time. However, much to its later regret, IBM turned this down also. Xerography is the process that Xerox perfected into its enormously successful line of plain-paper copiers.

In 1952, IBM introduced its first production computer, the 701. Since then, IBM has introduced several generations of computers, which have dominated the marketplace.

It isn't widely recognized, but in the Sixties, IBM management in effect bet the company on a new line of computers. Management recognized that to maintain domination of the market in the face of increasing competition a new generation of computers was necessary. In a four-year time span, the company spent 2½ times the amount spent on the Manhattan Project in World War II. It was the most massive privately financed corporate undertaking in history. The result was the 360 line of computers, which ensured IBM's domination for another decade.

Recently IBM has been undergoing another massive transformation. It is positioning itself to take advantage of the explosion that will take place in information processing in the Eighties.

IBM's great profit base has been in supplying data processing equipment to large organizations such as corporations and government agencies. Basically this has involved building large mainframe computers or, as we shall call them, "Cadillacs." However, recently great growth has occurred in the market for small computers known as minicomputers, or, as we shall call them, "Chevrolets." IBM missed out on the growth of this market in the Seventies. It also missed out on the market for personal computers or "Chevettes," as we shall call them.

IBM's strategy for the Eighties involves competing across the full range of opportunities in information processing including mainframes (Cadillacs), minicomputers (Chevrolets), and personal computers (Chevettes). In addition, it will compete in any new areas of information processing that look promising. The clear thrust of the strategy is that IBM intends to become nothing less than the General Motors of information processing in all its aspects. Previously it had essentially confined itself to the mainframe or Cadillac end of the industry.

To carry out its strategy, IBM has built enormous new automated facilities to give it the lowest cost of production. It is opening retail stores, licensing distributors such as Sears, and implementing direct-response marketing capabilities using mail-order and 800 telephone numbers to give it a low-cost distribution system for its new products. In addition, it has restructured its management to enable its executives to focus more effectively on specific market segments. The company, in modified form, is taking the organizational and product ideas that made General Motors for years America's most profitable corporation and adapting them to the information processing industry.

Will IBM's strategy work? We believe that it will. Considering IBM's resources and past history, it would be foolish to bet against the company.

The one cloud on the horizon is the government's antitrust suit that is still proceeding against the company. Paradoxically, from the shareholders' point of view, it probably doesn't matter if the government wins. The total market value of the pieces that would result from a split-up of IBM would probably greatly exceed the value of the current undivided company.

CHAPTER 5
ALCOA

RETURN ON BOOK VALUE	PAYOUT RATIO	PRICE/EARNINGS RATIO
71–80 High: 24.5%	71–80 High: 74%	71–80 High: 29
71–80 Low: 4.2%	71–80 Low: 18%	71–80 Low: 3
Assumed: 12.5%	Assumed: 30%	Assumed: 16

1981 Beginning Book Value per Share: $39.25

THE ENORMOUS RISE in energy costs has placed the aluminum industry in a very favorable position. Since aluminum production requires tremendous amounts of electricity, fewer aluminum plants will be built in the future (aluminum production uses approximately 4 percent of the electricity produced in the United States). At the same time, demand for aluminum is increasing, owing to its light weight. It is estimated that every pound of aluminum used in an automobile saves three gallons of gasoline over the life of the car. The net effect of these factors is that the industry should see demand growing faster than supply for the next decade at least. Alcoa, as the world's leading producer of aluminum products, is well positioned to benefit from this favorable situation.

Based upon the method outlined in Chapter 1 of Part II, we project that Alcoa stock will rise in price from $26 to $153 a share by the end of the decade—an increase of 488 percent.

Aluminum forms one-twelfth of the earth's crust. Yet for such an abundant material, it used to command an enormous price. An ounce of aluminum was worth more than an ounce of gold. The reason is that pure aluminum was extremely difficult to obtain. In its natural state, aluminum appears in combination with other elements, primarily oxygen. Separating it from oxygen was an extraordinarily expensive undertaking until 1886.

In 1886, Charles Hall, a twenty-two-year-old graduate of Oberlin College, discovered a revolutionary process for producing pure aluminum economically. He discovered that by running an electric current through aluminum oxide dissolved in a chemical solution he could produce pure aluminum pellets. Hall obtained a patent on his process and sought backing to begin commercial production. With the assistance of several investors, he formed the Pittsburgh Reduction Company in 1888.

Despite a monopoly on aluminum production, Hall's company faced great obstacles. Standarized metallurgical and fabricating techniques did not exist for aluminum as they did for other metals. In addition, it initially cost Hall almost $5 to produce a pound of aluminum; at the time, copper sold for 18 cents a pound and steel for 4 cents. Unable to convince manufacturing concerns to use aluminum in their products, Hall was forced to create novelty items—aluminum matchboxes, dog-collar decorations, and combs. He even produced aluminum playing cards on the theory that outdoor card players would find them attractive since they would be unaffected by weather and wouldn't blow away.

Hall's company slid into debt because of slow sales, and he approached Andrew Mellon, Pittsburgh's leading venture capitalist, for a $4,000 loan. Mellon was intrigued by aluminum's potential. It is light in weight, resists corrosion, is nontoxic, is workable, is strong, and is a good conductor of heat and electricity. After visiting Hall's little smelting plant, Mellon told Hall that a mere $4,000 would not do. Instead, he advanced the company $25,000 in exchange for stock, and his bank agreed to finance most of the young company's needs.

The company set up a plant in Niagara Falls, New York, becoming the first industrial user of the first major hydroelectric development in America. Hall continued to improve his process and reduced the cost of aluminum to 78 cents a pound by 1893. As the price dropped, new uses were found. By 1937, improvements in production processes had reduced the price of aluminum to 20 cents a pound. It sells for around 72 cents per pound today.

By 1946, Aluminum Company of America, as the company was now called, controlled over 90 percent of the aluminum business. In that year, however, the company was forced by the United States government to divest itself of its Canadian subsidiary, Alcan, and to license its aluminum-processing technology to its competitors. It now controls around 15 percent of the free world's aluminum supply.

In recent years, Alcoa has emphasized profitability. Unlike many American heavy industry companies, Alcoa, for the most part, has been able to generate sufficient cash internally to pay for its new plant and equipment. This ability is particularly beneficial in an era of high interest rates.

In order to reduce its vulnerability to cutoffs of either electricity or bauxite (the ore that aluminum is produced from), Alcoa has diversified geographically. New facilities have been built in Australia and Brazil.

One of Alcoa's more exciting developments is a new smelting process which, when perfected, may reduce by almost 50 percent the amount of electricity needed to produce aluminum.

CHAPTER 6
U.S. STEEL

RETURN ON BOOK VALUE	PAYOUT RATIO	PRICE/EARNINGS RATIO
71–80 High: 16.7%	71–80 High: 134%	71–80 High: 30
71–80 Low: Deficit	71–80 Low: Deficit	71–80 Low: Deficit
Assumed: 10.0%	Assumed: 45%	Assumed: 6.5

1981 Beginning Book Value per Share: $59.98

U NLIKE 3M OR IBM, U.S. Steel has very little control over its own destiny. Its prosperity, to a very large extent, depends on the actions of the United States government. Fortunately for both U.S. Steel and Bethlehem Steel, the government is finally adopting policies that should be beneficial to the American steel industry. The Reagan tax cut has greatly liberalized depreciation rules, and anti-dumping laws are likely to be strictly enforced.

Those who doubt the paramount importance of government policy to the health of the steel industry have only to look at Canada. Canada has perhaps the healthiest and most efficient steel industry in the world. Why? One reason is that Canada has extremely favorable laws regarding depreciation. Fast depreciation saves on taxes and therefore provides companies with the cash necessary to upgrade their facilities. A major Canadian steel company recently built an ultra-efficient new steel mill and was able to depreciate the plant over two years. In the United States, such a plant under pre-1980 tax laws would have been depreciated over fourteen years.

In addition, the Canadian government has vigorously enforced anti-dumping laws. European steel companies are subsidized by their governments as a matter of national policy. These governments are committed to maintaining employment in their steel industries. If a subsidized European company can sell a ton of steel in the United States, it will do so even though the price is below what it costs the company to make it. The reason is that the sale reduces the subsidy that the company requires from its government. The government only has to pay the difference between the price and the cost of production and not the full wage cost of the steel.

The entire blame for U.S. Steel's problems, however, does not rest with the government. In previous years, management was notably resistant to new ideas and made numerous mistakes. Management was oriented toward remaining Number One and did not give sufficient emphasis to profitability. Many marginal plants were retained. The attitudes of management were, to an extent, a legacy of U.S. Steel's complacent past.

U.S. Steel was born as a means to bring peace to the steel industry. Andrew Carnegie was not one to back down from a fight. After the Spanish-American War, his Carnegie Steel broke a gentlemen's agreement not to lower the price of steel rails. While Carnegie was away in Scotland on an extended vacation, his chief competitors, Federal Steel and National Tube (both controlled by J. P. Morgan), arranged with American Steel and Wire (controlled by "Bet-A-Million" Gates) and the "Tin Plate Trust" (controlled by "Judge" Moore) to wage an undeclared war on Carnegie. Gates's company, which had previously bought most of its steel from the Carnegie company, announced that it would henceforth seek new sources of supply. The Tin Plate Trust made a similar announcement. In addition, the Morgan-controlled railroads doubled their freight rates on Carnegie shipments.

Upon learning of these developments, Carnegie returned to Pittsburgh and announced that he would build the largest and most modern steel tube plant in the world on Lake Erie, thereby competing directly with National Tube. He also began negotiations to extend a local railroad that he owned to the Atlantic Coast, bypassing the Morgan-dominated railroads.

In the midst of these actions, Charles Schwab gave a speech at a dinner in New York City in which he passionately expounded on the benefits that would arise if the steel industry could be unified. J. P. Morgan was at the dinner and was so impressed by the speech that he asked Schwab, Carnegie Steel's president, to take a message to Andrew Carnegie indicating that the Morgan interests were prepared to buy his company out. Carnegie himself would have preferred to keep his company privately owned. But his executives were anxious to realize the cash that they had tied up in the company. Carnegie had recruited an exceptionally able staff of executives by arranging for them to own an interest in his firm. However, they could only sell their stock back to the company at a contractually set price. This repurchase price was far below the fair market value of the shares. Many of the executives were anxious to enjoy the good life and thus put great pressure on Carnegie to sell the company to Morgan.

Carnegie set a price of $492 million for the company, which Morgan readily agreed to pay. Morgan then arranged for Carnegie Steel, Federal Steel, National Tube, American Steel and Wire, the Tin Plate Trust, and several other companies to be combined into the U.S. Steel Corporation, with a capitalization of almost $1.5 billion. This was by far the largest corporation formed up until that time (1901).

Several months after the formation of U.S. Steel was complete, Morgan and Carnegie reputedly met in passing. Carnegie is supposed to have asked Morgan if he would have paid $100 million more for Carnegie Steel. Morgan without hesitation replied, "Yes." Upset at having sold too cheaply, Carnegie sulked for weeks afterward.

Charles Schwab, Carnegie's lieutenant, became the first president of the company. He left, however, three years later and joined Bethlehem Steel. Judge Gary, a conservative and unimaginative executive, replaced Schwab and remained in control of the company for over twenty years.

In the year of its inception, U.S. Steel produced almost two-thirds of America's steel. It was, however, saddled with a number of obsolete plants, a topheavy capital structure, and a conservative management after Schwab left. The company's weaknesses, for many years, were concealed by the enormous growth of the American economy, which created an almost insatiable demand for steel. Lacking effective foreign competition, company executives became complacent and were reluctant to innovate.

In the 1950s, U.S. Steel stock was one of the star performers in the stock market. The company benefited from a buoyant postwar economy plus the fact that the war had devastated European and Japanese steelmakers. By the 1960s, however, growth in steel demand had slowed, and Europe and Japan had rebuilt modern, efficient steel plants. The long ordeal of U.S. Steel had begun.

Current management at U.S. Steel appears to be much more realistic and practical than in previous administrations. Managers have closed a number of obsolete facilities and are focusing on profitability rather than on remaining Number One in terms of steel sales. When confronted with a production problem that they could not solve, they did the previously unthinkable—they asked a Japanese steel company for help. They are aggressively pursuing opportunities in chemicals and oil field equipment. Excess assets are being sold off. The company recently sold surplus coal properties and realized $750 million. These coal properties had been sitting underutilized for decades.

Effective management alone, however, will not restore U.S. Steel to adequate profitability. Only favorable government policies can do that. Fortunately for the company's long-suffering stockholders, these policies are in place.

Based upon the method outlined in Chapter 1 of Part II, we project that U.S. Steel stock will rise in price from $29 to $60 a share by the end of the decade—an increase of 107 percent.

CHAPTER 7
BETHLEHEM STEEL

RETURN ON BOOK VALUE	PAYOUT RATIO	PRICE/EARNINGS RATIO
71–80 High: 15.2%	71–80 High: 58%	71–80 High: 12
71–80 Low: Deficit	71–80 Low: Deficit	71–80 Low: Deficit
Assumed: 10.0%	Assumed: 40%	Assumed: 5.5

1981 Beginning Book Value per Share: $59.89

WHY WOULD A forty-one-year-old man, in 1903, give up a job that paid him $2 million a year (the equivalent of $20 million today)? This is the question that the financial community asked when Charles Schwab left his position as president of U.S. Steel in 1903.

Upon becoming president of U.S. Steel, Schwab, a hard worker, had strained himself even further to make the new company a success. The result was that his health failed, and, upon the advice of his doctor, he took a lengthy summer vacation aboard a rented yacht. The yacht stopped at Monte Carlo, where Schwab visited the gaming tables several times. Enterprising reporters, always alert for a good story, soon filled the newspapers with stories of how the president of United States Steel was "trying to break the bank at Monte Carlo."

J. P. Morgan was upset that the president of the company was attracting unfavorable attention. Upon Schwab's return, Morgan requested a meeting and expressed his displeasure. Morgan also indicated that in a large organization it was necessary that there be checks and balances and that Schwab would no longer have an entirely free hand. Used to running the operation his own way, Schwab resigned.

Schwab immediately purchased a small but sound steelmaking firm, Bethlehem Steel, and set about expanding it. He soon demonstrated the astuteness that had led to his meteoric rise to the top of Carnegie Steel. Schwab sold his interest in Bethlehem to the much larger but financially precarious U.S. Shipbuilding Company in exchange for bonds in that firm. The financial community thought Schwab was a fool for selling a sound company in exchange for bonds in a shaky firm. But the astute Schwab knew what he was doing. United States Shipbuilding soon failed as he had foreseen, and Schwab, holding bonds with voting rights, assumed complete control. He then sold off the weak assets and emerged controlling the second-largest steel company in America.

In one of his earlier decisions at Bethlehem, Schwab had committed large sums to building a huge plant to make a new type of structural steel that had been rejected by the more conservative U.S. Steel. This gamble proved to be a bonanza as architects soon specified this type of steel for skyscrapers that were being erected in increasing numbers.

In 1913, Schwab expanded Bethlehem by purchasing two other steel companies. His timing was again perfect, as, with the commencement of World War I, demand for steel skyrocketed. Bethlehem became the leading supplier of munitions to England. So important was Bethlehem to the English war effort that Germany reportedly offered Bethlehem $100 million cash if it would stop supplying England. By the end of World War I, Bethlehem had become the largest munitions manufacturer in the world, surpassing even Germany's Krupp Works. After the war, Schwab gradually withdrew from active management of Bethlehem, becoming, in effect, a senior statesman.

Unfortunately, Schwab's successors did not display his astuteness in dealing with steel's problems. Bethlehem, like U.S. Steel, was very slow in adapting to unfavorable government policies and the challenge of foreign competition.

In recent years, however, Bethlehem has begun to confront its problems aggressively. It has closed several marginal properties, and it is reviewing its coal and other surplus assets for possible sale.

Should Reagan's economic policies lead to a "reindustrialization" of the United States, Bethlehem will be a major beneficiary. The bulk of its output is geared to supplying the needs of heavy industry.

Based upon the method outlined in Chapter 1 of Part II, we project that Bethlehem stock will rise in price from $22 to $53 a share by the end of the decade—an increase of 141 percent.

CHAPTER 8
GENERAL
ELECTRIC

RETURN ON BOOK VALUE	PAYOUT RATIO	PRICE/EARNINGS RATIO
71–80 High: 21.6%	71–80 High: 53%	71–80 High: 26
71–80 Low: 15.8%	71–80 Low: 41%	71–80 Low: 7
Assumed: 17.0%	Assumed: 45%	Assumed: 16.5

1981 Beginning Book Value per Share: $35.67

"PROGRESS IS our most important product" was the slogan of the General Electric Company for many years. It symbolized the company's commitment to technological excellence. However, stung by losses in computers and nuclear power, GE became conservative and cut back on investments in technology and product quality in the Seventies. Its financially oriented chairman concentrated on wringing profits out of existing businesses. Rather than investing heavily in leading-edge technology, GE bought a coal company.

During this period, GE committed a grievous error. It allowed the quality of its consumer products to deteriorate. It "milked" them of profits to devote to other areas. Such a strategy might have been acceptable if GE had been preparing to abandon that area. But since it apparently intends to remain a factor in consumer products, its damaged reputation among the public will ultimately cost it far more than the short-run extra profits it made. This was a classic case in which company executives succumbed to pressure and adopted a "quick fix."

Now, however, General Electric apparently has recognized

129

that it must produce innovative, high-quality products if it is to grow and prosper. One sign of this recognition is that the company has promoted a "product man" to be its new chairman. The new chairman rose to his position by developing a billion-dollar engineered-plastics business from scratch for GE. Trained as a chemical engineer, he has a background that should allow him to feel more comfortable in making technological decisions.

One of the great weaknesses of American business in recent years has been the promotion of large numbers of lawyers and financial men to the top positions in corporations. These men are well equipped to deal with government and money problems, but their training tends to make them conservative and unwilling to take risks. Since developing innovative new products requires taking technological risks, many American companies have lagged behind their more adventuresome Japanese counterparts for this reason. GE, Du Pont, and several other major companies have apparently come to this conclusion and have recently installed technically trained "product men" in their top executive positions.

Based upon the method outlined in Chapter 1 of Part II, we project that General Electric stock will rise in price from $55 to $205 a share by the end of the decade—an increase of 273 percent.

One of the developments that will fuel this rise is the company's emphasis on the "factory of the future." GE is developing a full range of products including numerically controlled machines, computer-aided design systems, and industrial robots that can be used to totally automate a plant—from design of the product to its final manufacture. Experience in its own plants has shown that such equipment dramatically raises productivity along with product quality.

GE is also aggressively pursuing battery technology in an attempt to develop a practical electric car. Other growth areas that it is working on are medical electronics and genetic engineering. GE has received a patent on a bacterium that eats oil spills. This was the first patent issued on a new life form by the U.S. Patent Office.

We have no doubt that General Electric will recover from its mistakes in the Seventies. After all, the company owes its birth to a mistake by Thomas Edison. Edison believed that direct current (DC) was the basis on which the electric industry should be developed. Consequently, his company, the Edison Electric Light Company, committed itself to direct current. Unfortunately, by 1892, it was apparent that alternating current (AC) was to be the basis for the electric industry. Recognizing the impasse that the Edison Company had come to, J. P. Morgan arranged for it to merge with its equally large competitor, Thomson-Houston Electric Company.

The combined company, christened General Electric, was free to expand vigorously into AC generating systems, while honoring Edison's commitment to DC. The merged company also resolved several patent difficulties. Until the merger, neither company could build an efficient generating system without infringing on the other's patents.

Aided by the powerful Morgan interests and astute management, General Electric prospered. Under Charles Steinmetz, "the wizard of electricity," General Electric established a major industrial laboratory at Schenectady, New York, which produced a steady stream of useful inventions. The company electrified the locks at the Panama Canal, and its electric locomotives allowed the approaches to New York City's Grand Central Terminal to be covered over to form Park Avenue.

In 1919, at the request of the Navy, General Electric and Westinghouse joined forces to create the Radio Corporation of America. The government was concerned that the foreign-dominated Marconi Company might end up controlling American radio communications. In 1930, the government forced General Electric and Westinghouse to divest their RCA stock.

If the government had not intervened, GE might have ended up controlling a large part of the electric utility industry. In 1905, GE had begun to acquire utilities through its holding company, Electric Bond and Share. In 1924, under the threat of an antitrust action, GE abandoned the electric utility business.

In the Twenties, GE went into consumer appliances. This rapidly expanding business helped the company survive the Depression. At the close of World War II, the company was asked by the government to build turbine engines for the first U.S. jet plane. This contract led to the development of a sizable aircraft engine business.

During the Fifties, GE rode the postwar boom to unprecedented prosperity. Its stock rose over 600 percent during that decade.

CHAPTER 9
EASTMAN KODAK

RETURN ON BOOK VALUE	PAYOUT RATIO	PRICE/EARNINGS RATIO
71–80 High: 23.8%	71–80 High: 54%	71–80 High: 44
71–80 Low: 16.0%	71–80 Low: 41%	71–80 Low: 6
Assumed: 18.5%	Assumed: 45%	Assumed: 25

1981 Beginning Book Value per Share: $37.27

ASED UPON THE method outlined in Chapter 1 of Part II, we project that Kodak stock will rise in price from $65 to $374 a share by the end of the decade—an increase of 475 percent.

George Eastman had been raised in a poor family. He had quit school at fourteen to help support his widowed mother and two sisters. He worked first as an errand boy, then as a clerk, and finally as a bookkeeper in a bank. He explained the circumstances which led to the founding of his photographic company in the following way:

> . . . My superior, whose assistant I was, left the bank. The thing that I expected was that I should naturally fall in line for promotion. I didn't get it. Some relative of a director of the bank was brought in and placed over me. It wasn't right. It wasn't fair. I stayed for a short time longer, then quit. I gave myself up entirely to the work of cultivating my hobby, photography.

Eastman's first innovation in photography was a chemical coating which allowed pictures to be taken on a dry plate. Unfortunately, Eastman was unable to mass-produce his process.

133

Thwarted, he went overseas and returned with the rights to a process of making dry plates that had been invented in England. Using the English process, he built a successful business making dry plates. When competition in the manufacture of dry plates became fierce, one of Eastman's employees succeeded in placing the dry-plate emulsion on a fine-grained paper, and the era of photo-film arrived.

Other advances followed. In 1884, the company introduced film on rolls. Four years later, the first Kodak camera appeared, containing film for a hundred pictures. When the pictures had been taken, the entire camera was sent back to the factory for development. The finished pictures were returned along with the reloaded camera.

Eastman himself coined the name "Kodak," twice making use of his favorite letter, K. His affection for the letter apparently came from his mother, whose maiden name was Killowne.

The fundamental factor in Eastman's success was his obsession with making the complicated process of photography simple and inexpensive. He described his process of evaluating new photographic advances in the following way:

> There's no mystery about it. When the men bring me some development, we gather around and discuss it. Presently I am likely to hear someone say:
> "That's fine. Amazing how intricate it is, yet it works."
> Then I say, "Boys, we have failed. Let's do it over again."
> We do it again—and perhaps again—until I hear someone exclaim:
> "How simple."
> Then I know we have succeeded.

Eastman was one of the first American manufacturers to emphasize large-scale production to create low unit costs. To sell his enormous output, he spent millions on advertising, making Kodak one of the most recognized trade names in the world.

Eastman was uncompromising when it came to product quality. He invested heavily in research to ensure that Kodak's products remained the finest in the world.

The executives that have followed Eastman have maintained

his commitment to excellence. They have spent heavily on research and development and have resisted temptations to reduce quality for short-term earnings gains. In 1980, Kodak spent over $520 million on research and development.

In the Seventies, Kodak's earnings stayed on a plateau for a while as it attempted to bring two major products on stream at the same time—its high-volume Ektaprint dry copier and its instant camera. Since then profits have grown strongly. Even in 1979 when silver prices were soaring, Kodak managed to increase earnings. Since Kodak uses approximately 50 million ounces of silver each year, for every $1 that silver rose in price Kodak's costs rose by $50 million.

For the future Kodak is introducing advanced products for the health industry. Its new Ektachem blood analyzer utilizes a new method of analyzing blood serum. The company is also at work on processes that reduce the amount of radiation required to take X-rays. Advances in microfilm technology are also under development.

There is speculation that Kodak is at work on a revolutionary new camera system. Kodak is extremely secretive about its new products, but in England it has published documents indicating that it is at work on a camera that uses film "disks" instead of strips. If Kodak does introduce a new camera system, it should be very beneficial to the company's profits. The Instamatic and pocket Instamatic camera systems produced enormous earnings gains after they were fully introduced.

CHAPTER 10
INTERNATIONAL PAPER

RETURN ON BOOK VALUE	PAYOUT RATIO	PRICE/EARNINGS RATIO
71–80 High: 23.4%	71–80 High: 96%	71–80 High: 27
71–80 Low: 7.0%	71–80 Low: 29%	71–80 Low: 5
Assumed: 11.0%	Assumed: 40%	Assumed: 16

1981 Beginning Book Value per Share: $56.66

REAL ESTATE HAS long been considered to be an excellent inflation hedge. During the Seventies, most real estate properties increased greatly in price. U.S. timberland, as one would expect, was no exception. During the Seventies, for example, southern pine timberland appreciated at a rate 3 percent above inflation.

Given these facts, what do you think happened to the price of shares in America's largest private landowner in the 1970s? This is a company that owns outright approximately 7.5 million acres of U.S. timberland, much of it southern pine timberland. In 1981, after a decade of virulent inflation in the United States, International Paper common stock is selling below what it sold for in 1969. This is perhaps the clearest example of how pessimistic investors in common stocks have become in the last decade. They have ignored what is clearly an enormous rise in the underlying asset value of International Paper.

Part of the explanation with respect to International Paper's poor stock market performance is that the company has not attempted to engage in a "quick fix" to boost its earnings dramati-

136

cally for a few quarters. Instead, the company's management has actually retarded short-term earnings in favor of an enhanced long-term outlook. Their most crucial decision was to extend the cutting cycle on their southern timberlands from twenty or twenty-five years to thirty or thirty-five years. By extending the cutting cycle ten years, they have reduced the wood they have available in the short run. But in that extra ten years, trees that could be used only for pulp grow big enough to be used as timber, and trees as timber are worth three to six times more than they are as pulp. Clearly it is worthwhile to wait. And that's just what International Paper's management has decided to do in spite of pressures to generate short-term earnings.

In other recent decisions, the company sold off its General Crude subsidiary for $800 million. The subsidiary needed cash for development that International Paper thought could be better employed in its wood products business. International Paper retains the mineral rights on most of its lands. It has an agreement with Mobil allowing Mobil to explore for oil and gas on its lands in exchange for up to a 25 percent royalty. Thus far Mobil's exploration has not yielded significant results.

International Paper is also rationalizing its operations. It is trading lands that are located far from its plants for properties that are closer and thereby cutting transportation costs. It is also investing heavily in new plants to lower its operating costs.

Another favorable long-range development for International Paper is its extensive planting of "Supertrees." Supertrees are genetically improved strains of trees that grow faster and produce more wood. Today an acre of thirty-five-year-old southern pine will produce about 8,500 board feet of sawtimber. An acre of Supertrees will produce 15,000 board feet in just thirty years, a dramatic improvement. It will, however, take many years for the company to reap the full benefit of planting Supertrees.

Based upon the method outlined in Chapter 1 of Part II, we project that International Paper stock will rise in price from $42 to $166 a share by the end of the decade—an increase of 295 percent.

International Paper began, in 1898, as a merger of eighteen paper companies located in the northeastern United States with tongue-twisting names such as Winnipiseogee and Umbagog. It initially controlled over a million acres of land and was primarily a newsprint manufacturer.

In the early 1920s, the company expanded into Canada in search of low-cost wood and power, the key ingredients in papermaking. It acquired cutting rights on millions of acres. The elimination of U.S. tariffs on newsprint had made this expansion feasible.

As a consequence of its need for water for its paper mills, the company developed several hydroelectric projects and became a significant supplier of electricity. At one point, the company was named International Paper and Power Corporation. However, the company divested itself of its hydroelectric plants in the face of growing legal problems and government regulation and in 1941 reverted to the name International Paper Company.

In the late Twenties and Thirties, the company expanded into the South and pioneered in the development of kraft paper and paperboards. It also acquired millions of acres of southern timberland at exceptionally favorable prices.

Beginning in the Forties, the company became more heavily involved in packaging. It acquired companies making milk cartons, folding cartons, and labels. The company also entered into the lumber and plywood business.

Today International Paper is an integrated producer of wood products with a primary emphasis on paper.

CHAPTER 11
TEXACO

RETURN ON BOOK VALUE	PAYOUT RATIO	PRICE/EARNINGS RATIO
71–80 High: 21.2%	71–80 High: 65%	71–80 High: 12
71–80 Low: 9.2%	71–80 Low: 29%	71–80 Low: 3
Assumed: 12.0%	Assumed: 45%	Assumed: 7.5

1981 Beginning Book Value per Share: $46.64

JOHN "BET-A-MILLION" GATES was a man who loved to gamble. Once at the dinner table, two flies landed on a cube of sugar. Gates bet $1,000 that the fly on the left would take off before the one on the right. He also used to amuse himself while traveling by train by betting thousands of dollars on which raindrop would reach the bottom of the windowpane first.

Gates had acquired the wherewithal to make his unusual bets in the barbed-wire business. He was the man who convinced skeptical Texans of the benefits of barbed wire in 1878. Realizing that more was needed than his statement that his barbed wire was "light as air, stronger than whiskey, and cheaper than dirt," Gates conceived a masterful promotion to sell it. He built a corral of the wire and challenged local ranchers to bring their meanest steers. After a preliminary rodeo, forty steers were herded into the corral and stampeded. Bouncing off the barbed wire, the bruised and bewildered animals soon stood still. The ranchers were convinced and orders rushed in. Gates eventually created a "Barbed Wire Trust" (American Steel and Wire), which he sold to J. P. Morgan for inclusion in U.S. Steel.

139

One of Gates's biggest bets occurred in 1902, when he decided to back an oil man named Joseph Cullinan. Cullinan, a former Standard Oil employee, was one of the first to recognize the potential of the 1901 oil discovery at Spindletop near the Texas coast. He realized that this discovery offered a chance to build a major American oil company. Up until then, Standard Oil had a virtual monopoly on American oil and would have controlled Spindletop had Texas not been one of the first states to pass antitrust laws which effectively barred the Rockefeller interests.

Obtaining initial backing from a group of Texans and a New York financier, Cullinan began building his company. Gates owned a piece of land in Port Arthur, Texas, which Cullinan wanted to build a refinery on, and the two met to discuss the sale of the land. Gates was so impressed with Cullinan that he offered to invest heavily in the larger consolidated firm that Cullinan was contemplating. Thus when the Texas Company was formed by Cullinan in 1902, Gates was a major stockholder.

Gates's judgment of Cullinan proved to be correct. Cullinan expanded the Texas Company rapidly. By 1904, it was producing 5 percent of America's oil. Cullinan, however, was an autocratic manager. He once accepted leadership of a firefighting crew at an oil well only on the condition that he could shoot anyone who disobeyed his orders. In 1913, after Gates's death, Cullinan was forced out by the other stockholders.

Cullinan, however, continued to vindicate Gates's judgment. He formed a smaller oil company that returned $360,000 over a thirteen-year period for each original $100 share. None of this, however, benefited Texas Company shareholders.

In the 1930s, the Texas Company proved that it had inherited Gates's and Cullinan's luck. Standard Oil of California gave it a half interest in its prolific Saudi Arabian oil concession in exchange for capital and marketing help. Assured of a source of cheap crude, the Texas Company concentrated on developing its already extensive marketing system and minimized further exploration. Selling gasoline in all fifty states, it became America's most profitable large oil company. It changed its name to Texaco in 1959. Texaco had long been its cable address.

Unfortunately for Texaco stockholders, the company's long period of success had developed an autocratic management which resisted change. When the era of cheap crude ended in the early Seventies, Texaco was slow to adapt. It was stuck with an inefficient marketing system and declining production from its U.S. oil and gas properties. Only with a new top management in the last year has Texaco begun to confront its problems aggressively. To expand its exploration program, it has decentralized decision-making, and it is entering into joint venture arrangements with several successful small oil exploration companies. It is shrinking its marketing system to a more efficient size by withdrawing from several states.

For the future, Texaco is establishing a strong position in alternative sources of energy. It has established a leading position in coal-gasification technology. Six different coal-gasification projects are now under review. It also is a participant in a shale-oil project. In a joint venture with CPC International, Texaco is building a plant which will produce sixty million gallons of fuel-grade ethanol each year from corn.

Based upon the method outlined in Chapter 1 of Part II, we project that Texaco stock will rise in price from $35 to $70 a share by the end of the decade—an increase of 100 percent.

CHAPTER 12
MERCK

RETURN ON BOOK VALUE	PAYOUT RATIO	PRICE/EARNINGS RATIO
71–80 High: 29.8%	71–80 High: 63%	71–80 High: 45
71–80 Low: 24.1%	71–80 Low: 39%	71–80 Low: 11
Assumed: 20.5%	Assumed: 45%	Assumed: 28

1981 Beginning Book Value per Share: $24.64

I N EXPLAINING THE wide range of research that his drug company engaged in, George Merck II frequently emphasized the role that "serendipity" played: "Remember the story of the Three Princes of Serendip who went out looking for treasure. They didn't find what they were looking for, but they kept finding other things just as valuable. That's serendipity, and our business is full of it." Recently Merck scientists thought they were on the trail of a new way to control high blood pressure but ended up instead with a treatment for glaucoma.

Through its emphasis on research, Merck is in the fortunate position of being able to control its own destiny to a large extent. As long as it continues to develop profitable new drugs, the company will grow regardless of the state of the economy or the actions of its competitors. Despite its $3 billion size, Merck has plenty of room to grow. It controls only about 5 percent of the U.S. drug market and less than 1 percent of some major world markets.

Unlike some other American drug companies, Merck has continued to spend increasing amounts on research. It has done so to maintain its preeminent position in the face of strong competition from German, Swiss, and Japanese drug makers.

To meet the challenge of increased foreign competition, Merck

142

has redirected the basis of its research programs. Under its old approach, the company used to randomly screen thousands of chemical compounds in the search for a new drug. Now it is concentrating on determining exactly how a particular disease process operates and then tailoring a substance to alter that process. The company is also making a substantial commitment to research in genetic engineering.

Merck markets its drugs on a worldwide basis. It has done this to spread the costs of its research program over a larger sales volume. It can cost over $50 million to develop a single drug to the point where it can be marketed in the United States. A large part of this cost results from U.S. government regulations. In the last decade, the average time needed to satisfy U.S. Food and Drug Administration regulations has increased from two to eight years. One result of this increased delay in approval is that a new drug is effectively protected by patents for only ten years instead of the seventeen provided by law. Currently, there is a bill in Congress to allow drug companies seventeen years patent protection from the date the drug is approved and not the date it is discovered. If the bill is passed, it should stimulate increased research.

If Merck has a weakness, it is that it tends to rely almost entirely on its own internal research for new products. This practice keeps the morale of its researchers high, but the company may be overlooking profitable products by not seeking outside ideas.

Based upon the method outlined in Chapter 1 of Part II, we project that Merck stock will rise in price from $82 to $332 a share by the end of the decade—an increase of 305 percent.

The Merck tradition in pharmaceuticals extends back to 1688, when Friedrich Merck purchased At the Sign of the Angel, an apothecary in Germany. In the early 1800s, the business was expanded into manufacturing pharmaceuticals, with Merck becoming the first company to commercially produce morphine (1827), codeine (1836), and cocaine (1862).

Concerned that inferior products not manufactured by them were being sold in America, the firm sent George Merck to establish a branch in the United States in 1887. Initially, the American branch merely imported drugs and chemicals. It later began to manufacture them at a plant in Rahway, New Jersey.

During World War I, George Merck, who had become a natu-
ralized U.S. citizen in 1908, voluntarily turned over 80 percent
of the stock in the company to the Allied Property Custodian.
This stock represented the interest in the company that was held
by his relations in Germany. After the war, the company's finances were restructured in a way which eliminated the German
interests and left George Merck in control.

In 1925, George Merck's son became president. During his
tenure, the company played an important role in the discovery
and manufacture of many important drugs and vitamins. Five
outside scientists ultimately received Nobel Prizes for work done
in collaboration with Merck. Several vitamins, including B_1, B_2,
B_6, pantothenic acid, and B_{12}, were first synthesized by Merck
scientists alone or in collaboration with other scientists. The
company also played an important role in developing first the
sulfa drugs and then antibiotics. The first penicillin used to treat
an infection in the United States was made by Merck. Arthritis
sufferers have also benefited from Merck research. Company
scientists played an important role in the discovery of cortisone.

For many years, Merck confined itself to manufacturing the
basic ingredients that other pharmaceutical firms formulated,
packaged, and resold in finished form to druggists and physi-
cians. After World War II, competition forced Merck to become
a fully integrated drug firm. In 1953, it accomplished this task by
merging with Sharp and Dohme, a long-established Philadelphia
company that had an excellent reputation among doctors and
druggists. It also possessed an experienced force of salesmen.

In the Sixties and Seventies, the bulk of Merck's profits came
from drugs to treat chronic conditions such as arthritis and high
blood pressure. In the Eighties, this trend should continue.
Merck has a drug (MK-421) for controlling high blood pressure
which is in the early stage of testing. Some analysts believe this
could be a "billion-dollar drug." The company also has a very
promising antibiotic (MK-787) that apparently kills a wider range
of microbes than any other antibiotic developed to date. Animal
health will also be a significant revenue producer in the Eighties.
Merck has a new drug, Invomec, that has shown exceptional
promise for control of parasites in livestock.

CHAPTER 13
GENERAL FOODS

RETURN ON BOOK VALUE	PAYOUT RATIO	PRICE/EARNINGS RATIO
71–80 High: 20.2%	71–80 High: 63%	71–80 High: 20
71–80 Low: 15.4%	71–80 Low: 37%	71–80 Low: 5
Assumed: 15.0%	Assumed: 45%	Assumed: 12.5

1981 Beginning Book Value per Share: $32.58

C W. POST, the founder of what later became General Foods, hated coffee with a passion. He developed Postum to give people an alternative to it. Ironically, after he died, the corporation that he founded purchased a coffee company. Today, Post's corporation, General Foods, sells 40 percent of all the coffee sold in America under its Maxwell House, Sanka, Brim, and Maxim brands. Corporations do not always respect their founders' wishes.

If Post's health had not failed, he probably would have ended up as a successful manufacturer of farm implements. However, ill health forced him to sell his implement firm, in 1884, and begin an odyssey searching for a cure. By 1891, Post was in terrible shape and was carried by stretcher to Dr. John Kellogg's sanitarium in Battle Creek, Michigan. Here he was fed a special diet that included a hot cereal drink.

His health did not improve in the sanitarium, and as a last alternative, Post went to stay in the home of a Christian Scientist in Battle Creek. Almost immediately his health began to improve, and upon being cured he decided to open his own sanitarium. In his sanitarium, Post served the various health foods that he had found of value during his long search for a cure.

145

In 1895, Post began to market Monk's Brew, a hot cereal drink made of wheat and bran, browned and blended with molasses. It is thought that this drink probably was the same one he had been served at Dr. Kellogg's sanitarium. Sales of Monk's Brew were disappointing until Post changed its name to Postum. Initially he marketed it by brewing free samples at grocery stores. He then proceeded to advertise in newspapers. Until Post, food products were seldom advertised. With the help of massive advertising, Postum was a huge success. Post eventually became the largest single advertiser in the country.

In 1898, Post introduced Grape-Nuts. Grape-Nuts consisted of whole wheat and malted barley flours, mixed, raised, and baked for twenty hours. The long baking converted the starches to dextrose or grape sugar, the form all starches take in the digestive process. Grape-Nuts was thus a partially predigested food. Post advertised Grape-Nuts as a scientific food which made red blood redder.

In 1906, Post introduced Elijah's Manna. It was immediately denounced as sacrilegious. Post countered by noting: "Perhaps no one should eat angel food cake, enjoy Adam's Ale, live in St. Paul, nor work for Bethlehem Steel, nor could one have the healing benefits of St. Jacob's Oil, one should have his Adam's apple removed and never again name a child for the good people of the Bible." However, when sales didn't pick up, Post renamed the product Post Toasties. Under that name it became a huge success.

After Post's death in 1915, his Postum Cereal Company acquired many other food companies, including Jell-O (1925), Swans Down Cake Flour and Minute Tapioca (1926), Log Cabin Syrup (1927), and Maxwell House Coffee (1928).

Post's daughter, Marjorie Merriweather Post, was responsible for the acquisition of the Birds Eye frozen-food line. One day a frozen goose was brought aboard her yacht with other provisions. She was so impressed with the flavor and texture of the goose when it was served that she tracked down the supplier, Clarence Birdseye. Birdseye had discovered that quick freezing preserves the natural characteristics of food by preventing the formation of the large ice crystals that gather in slowly frozen food. It is these large crystals that rupture the cell structure and destroy the flavor, texture, and natural juices of food. Birdseye's business was purchased for $29 million in 1929, and the name General Foods was adopted for the corporation.

In the late Sixties, General Foods was carried away by hamburger mania and purchased the Burger Chef chain. The company has since lost large sums of money trying to make that business viable. In 1980, it was still operating at a loss. Undaunted by its experience with Burger Chef, General Foods is investing in several theme restaurants. Its Meriwether's restaurants are designed to resemble spacious English country homes. GuadalaHARRY's restaurants have a Mexican motif.

Despite its Burger Chef problems, General Foods is considered to be an astutely managed company. It has maintained the leadership of its major brands through aggressive advertising (it is the nation's second largest advertiser) and has continued to develop new products. In 1980, it introduced Oven-Fry, a coating mix for chicken which has been well received.

For the future, General Foods is looking for growth in its theme restaurants and overseas. It has the opportunity to substantially broaden the range of products that it offers in several countries. Growth is also expected to come from new products. In 1980, it invested almost $80 million in research and development.

One potential problem in the Eighties is a government study investigating the possibility that the solvent used by every U.S. decaffeinated coffee maker could be a cancer-producing agent. Minuscule residues of the solvent remain on the coffee beans after the decaffeination process. Should the report be unfavorable, General Foods' Sanka brand could be hurt. In the event of an unfavorable report, however, the company is prepared. In 1979, it bought HAG, the leading decaffeinated coffee company in Europe. HAG has developed an alternate technology which does not use the suspect solvent.

Based upon the method outlined in Chapter 1 of Part II, we project that General Foods stock will rise in price from $28 to $115 a share by the end of the decade—an increase of 311 percent.

CHAPTER 14
DU PONT

RETURN ON BOOK VALUE	PAYOUT RATIO	PRICE/EARNINGS RATIO
71–80 High: 20.5%	71–80 High: 78%	71–80 High: 25
71–80 Low: 7.5%	71–80 Low: 43%	71–80 Low: 6
Assumed: 14.5%	Assumed: 50%	Assumed: 15.5

1981 Beginning Book Value per Share: $39.26

D U PONT HAS A knack for being involved in deals that set records. Its recent purchase of Conoco was the largest and most widely publicized acquisition in American business annals. Yet nearly eighty years ago Du Pont itself was acquired in what must rank as the quietest and most profitable acquisition in history. In that transaction, the entire company was acquired for a cash outlay of $2,100.

The Du Pont Company can trace its origin to the founding of the "Establishment of a Manufacture of Military and Sporting Powder in the United States of America" in 1802. Supposedly Irénée du Pont, who had recently come to America to escape the French Revolution, went hunting one day with a friend. After running out of gunpowder he had brought with him from France, Irénée began using American gunpowder. Irénée found this powder to be so inferior that he decided to set up a powder manufacturing plant using a process that he had learned in France under Lavoisier, the great chemist. By the War of 1812, his company was the largest powder maker in the United States. Under family management, the Du Pont Company continued to be the major supplier of explosives to the U.S. government during the Civil War and the Spanish-American War.

In 1902, apparently lacking a family member qualified to run the business, the partners in the company decided to sell it for $12 million to the other major explosives manufacturer in the United States. Three young du Pont cousins, however, convinced the partners to sell the company to them for $12 million in bonds of a reorganized Du Pont Company plus 28 percent of its common stock. Amazingly enough, the only cash that the cousins had to come up with was $2,100, which was used to legally purchase the assets of the old company so that they could be transferred to the new company. In effect, the entire purchase price was to be paid out of the future profits of the company. So conservative was the accounting of the old company that its assets at the time of purchase were clearly worth at least $24 million. Considered in terms of percentage return on actual cash investment, this has to be the most lucrative acquisition in American business history.

One of the cousins involved in the transaction was Pierre S. du Pont. As head of the Du Pont Company's financial department, he developed new methods of asset accounting, capital allocation, financial forecasting, and determining a rate of return on invested capital. His techniques revolutionized the management of large corporate organizations. For his work, Pierre du Pont has been called "the architect of the modern corporation."

At the direction of Pierre du Pont, the Du Pont Company made its single most profitable investment. It purchased 28 percent of General Motors common stock at bargain prices. Pierre du Pont went on to set the policies that built General Motors into the world's largest industrial enterprise. Judging from the results that he achieved at both the Du Pont Company and General Motors, Pierre du Pont is clearly one of the greatest businessmen of the twentieth century.

In the Thirties, Du Pont scientists created nylon. This was to become the company's single most profitable product and led to the development of a huge artificial-fibers business. Unfortunately, Du Pont relied on its artificial-fibers business too long for growth. It failed to develop new products. Thus when the demand for artificial fibers collapsed in the Seventies, Du Pont fell upon hard times.

Now Du Pont has targeted life sciences as its major area for growth in the Eighties. It expects to get nearly half of its profits from agricultural chemicals, pharmaceuticals, and medical instruments by the end of the decade. A signal of the change at Du Pont is that a chemist will replace a lawyer as head of the company. The company is clearly emphasizing research. It has significantly boosted its spending on research and development to $480 million.

Du Pont is believed to have the largest genetic engineering research group of any chemical maker. Genetic engineering promises to revolutionize many of the processes by which chemicals are produced. Genetic engineering also has exciting promise as a means of developing new drugs and medicines. Considering what Du Pont laboratories have come up with in the past, it would not be surprising if they come up with a truly revolutionary product based on genetic engineering.

Du Pont has also taken steps to develop the more mundane side of its business. The acquisition of Conoco will provide the company with access to petroleum raw materials and protect it against further increases in the price of oil.

Based upon the method outlined in Chapter 1 of Part II, we project that Du Pont stock will rise in price from $39 to $154 a share by the end of the decade—an increase of 295 percent.

CHAPTER 15
GENERAL MOTORS

RETURN ON BOOK VALUE	PAYOUT RATIO	PRICE/EARNINGS RATIO
71–80 High: 23.6%	71–80 High: 104%	71–80 High: 17
71–80 Low: Deficit	71–80 Low: Deficit	71–80 Low: Deficit
Assumed: 14.0%	Assumed: 50%	Assumed: 8.5

1981 Beginning Book Value per Share: $61.49

THE JAPANESE ARE dominating American car manufacturers in the U.S. market. This is a widespread perception of the American auto industry. This perception, however, is not correct with respect to General Motors. The Japanese are not dominating GM. General Motors has maintained a consistent 45 percent share of the U.S. market in the past decade, and it is continuing to do so. The increased Japanese share of the U.S. market has come at the expense of Ford and Chrysler, not GM.

A remarkable transformation has occurred at General Motors in the last few years. From a complacent, unimaginative giant, the company has transformed itself into an aggressive technological leader. In a move unprecedented in industrial history, GM is committing $40 billion to totally renew its product line and its factories. The result of this revitalization will be that GM will have a completely redesigned, fuel-efficient line of cars manufactured in cost-effective plants. The X and the J cars are the first tangible evidence of this transformation. Still to come are the B and A cars and a three-cylinder minicar that may have a 60-mpg highway rating. Technologically, General Motors is now estimated to ᴜe at least a year and a half in advance of its American competition.

By choice, General Motors has not been a major factor in world auto markets. It has factories in many countries but it has concentrated its efforts on the United States. Now GM is gearing up for a worldwide attack. Stressing interchangeable parts manufactured worldwide but assembled in the local market, GM is developing a car to compete in the basic transportation market. GM's so-called world car is likely to do well against the Japanese. The Japanese automakers do not like to have plants located in foreign countries. They prefer to export from Japan. Since most governments want jobs to be created within their territory, GM, with its local factories, will have a substantial advantage.

One of the reasons Japanese cars have sold so well in the United States is their perceived higher quality. It isn't widely recognized, but a primary reason for this higher quality is that Japanese auto plants are much more highly automated than most U.S. plants. Industrial machines and robots are much less likely to make errors than human workers. In its new plants, GM is incorporating the latest in technology. As it gains production experience with its new line of cars, quality should begin to approach Japanese levels.

General Motors' strategy moves are surprising for a company of its size. In terms of worldwide sales, it is 50 percent bigger than Toyota, Nissan (Datsun), Toyo Kogyo (Mazda), and Honda combined. Yet it is moving with the aggressiveness of a small entrepreneurial organization.

General Motors was founded by William Durant. Durant has been called "America's greatest promoter not behind bars." A high school dropout, Durant, in 1903, gained control of the Flint Wagon Works. After obtaining the rights to manufacture a horseless carriage designed by David Buick, Durant raised $10 million and began production. Renamed the Buick Motor Company, the business proved to be highly profitable. Using the profits from Buick, Durant began buying up other major auto concerns, including Cadillac and Oldsmobile. He was convinced that the formula for success in the auto industry was a large corporation making a variety of models and controlling its own parts suppliers.

In 1908, Durant combined the various companies that he controlled into the General Motors Company. In 1909, he almost purchased the Ford Motor Company. Owing to tight money conditions which had crippled his young company, Henry Ford had agreed to sell his firm to Durant for $8 million. Durant pleaded with his bankers to lend him the money. But this time the "man who could coax a bird out of a tree" failed to coax his bankers out of a loan. The bankers were not convinced of the future of the auto industry. Their doubts, however, were misplaced. Within twenty years, the Ford Motor Company was worth $1 billion.

In 1910, Durant overextended the company financially, and he was forced to give up control to a voting trust directed by the company's bankers. Undaunted, in 1911 he joined forces with Louis Chevrolet, a Swiss-born former racecar driver for Buick, and formed a new company, the Chevrolet Motor Car Company. Their product, a low-priced car, competed successfully with Ford's Model T. Armed with profits from Chevrolet, Durant began quietly to accumulate voting trust certificates in GM. He also persuaded his friend John Raskob to purchase shares. It was Raskob who interested his boss, Pierre du Pont, in GM.

By 1916, Durant had acquired enough shares to take back control of GM from the bankers. He merged Chevrolet with the company and began an ambitious expansion plan. Its timing, unfortunately, coincided with the post–World War I depression, and Durant again lost control—this time to the Du Pont Company. At the direction of Pierre du Pont, the Du Pont Company had invested a sizable part of its profits from World War I in GM. If GM went bankrupt, not only would Du Pont's stock holdings become worthless, but it would lose a major customer. GM purchased substantial quantities of paint and varnish from Du Pont. Thus in order to protect its investment, Du Pont stepped in and rescued GM from the financial catastrophe brought on by Durant. The Du Pont Company ended up owning 28 percent of GM's stock.

Under Pierre du Pont's guidance, GM adopted the policies that made it, for many years, America's dominant company. Alfred Sloan is often given credit for these policies, but he only implemented them. In actuality, it was Pierre du Pont who originated them and who ordered that they be carried out. Pierre du Pont, however, disliked the limelight and preferred to operate in the background.

It was Pierre du Pont who introduced the structure of centralized control of policy and financial matters combined with decentralized operations. Investment decisions and operating results for the first time were judged in terms of return on total assets. Unlike Henry Ford, who believed that all Americans wanted only basic transportation in one form ("They can have any color they want as long as it's black," he said), Pierre du Pont realized that Americans had diverse needs that only a broad product line could supply. He thus established the policy that each GM division would be given a definite price bracket, with Chevrolet at the bottom and Cadillac at the top, so that the company had an offering for each type of customer. Annual model changes and varieties of colors for cars were introduced to maintain the interest of consumers.

The result of these changes was that GM surpassed the much larger Ford in the late Twenties and went on to become America's greatest corporation. Pierre du Pont had created such a brilliant structure that the corporation made enormous sums of money regardless of who was managing it.

In control of a money machine, GM executives basically allowed the business to run itself. They were content to follow trends in the automobile market rather than to innovate or take risks. Now, however, GM leadership has roused itself and, for the first time since Pierre du Pont, is committing the corporation to radical change. This strategy is not without risks. But to do nothing in the face of a changed marketplace would be even riskier.

Based upon the method outlined in Chapter 1 of Part II, we project that General Motors stock will rise in price from $46 to $126 a share by the end of the decade—an increase of 174 percent.

CHAPTER 16
EXXON

RETURN ON BOOK VALUE	PAYOUT RATIO	PRICE/EARNINGS RATIO
71–80 High: 25.3%	71–80 High: 56%	71–80 High: 13
71–80 Low: 13.1%	71–80 Low: 36%	71–80 Low: 4
Assumed: 16.0%	Assumed: 40%	Assumed: 8.5

1981 Beginning Book Value per Share: $29.41

THE STANDARD OIL Company of New Jersey had bad luck in the United States Supreme Court. In 1911, having found the company in violation of the antitrust laws, the Court ordered the company to, in effect, divest itself of all of its subsidiaries. Out of the dissolution, thirty-four separate companies emerged, including what are now Exxon, Ashland Oil, Mobil, Atlantic-Richfield, Conoco, Pennzoil, Chesebrough-Ponds, Marathon Oil, Standard Oil of California, Standard Oil of Indiana, and Standard Oil of Ohio. This stroke of bad luck for the company, however, proved to be highly rewarding for its shareholders. The market value of the separate companies whose stock was distributed to Standard's shareholders soon greatly exceeded the value of their old Standard Oil shares.

In 1969, the Supreme Court again dealt Standard Oil of New Jersey a blow when it refused to review a decision denying the company the right to use its Esso trademark nationwide. The Esso trademark is derived from the initials SO (standing for Standard Oil), and the other Standard Oil companies objected to Standard Oil of New Jersey's using the name in their trading areas. As a result, Esso could be used in only nineteen states. Elsewhere the company marketed under the Humble and Enco trade-

155

marks. It cost an estimated $100 million for the company to convert to the name Exxon, but the change allowed a unification of its marketing within the United States. The new name might also, company executives undoubtedly hope, bring the company better luck in the Supreme Court should it ever end up there again.

Despite its reverses in the Supreme Court, Exxon has become the world's largest industrial enterprise. In terms of sales ($110 billion in 1980), it is almost twice the size of General Motors. Its revenues are greater than the gross national product of Sweden.

Only very large oil discoveries ("elephants") will have a significant impact on a company as huge as Exxon. Consequently, Exxon has oriented its petroleum exploration toward the frontier areas. It participated in exploration in Alaska and the North Sea, and it has extensive exploration going on in Malaysia, Africa, the Canadian Arctic, and offshore in the United States. The strategy of hunting for "elephants" is risky, but the rewards will be enormous if Exxon finds a large pool of oil in a non-OPEC country. While Exxon, like most major oil companies, produced more oil than it has found in the past decade, it would take only one "elephant" to change the situation. In the meantime, the enormous rise in oil prices has dramatically boosted the value of Exxon's petroleum reserves. Using the SEC's method of calculating the value of oil reserves, Exxon's Book Value per Share is currently $110.

Exxon's management recently displayed uncharacteristic ineptness when it spent $1.2 billion to acquire Reliance Electric. Exxon's stated reason for acquiring Reliance was to give it the means to rapidly develop and market an energy-saving new technology for electric motors. Unfortunately, shortly after the acquisition, it was announced that the new technology wouldn't be economic to develop.

Based upon the method outlined in Chapter 1 of Part II, we project that Exxon stock will rise in price from $32 to $83 a share by the end of the decade—an increase of 159 percent.

Despite the presence of "New Jersey" in the old corporate name, Exxon was actually started in Cleveland, Ohio. John D. Rockefeller was a successful young commodity commission merchant in that city when an oil boom occurred not far away in western Pennsylvania. Rockefeller visited the booming region. The first thing that he noted was that new oil discoveries and cutthroat competitors could drive the price of oil downward at any time. Since the start of the boom in 1859, the price of oil had fallen from $20 to 10 cents a barrel.

Rockefeller concluded that refining was the only way to participate in the oil business. Only in that sector could he hope to control his own destiny. Oil at this time was mainly refined into kerosene to be used for illumination.

In 1863, he and a partner invested $4,000 in a refinery in Cleveland. Rockefeller cautiously expanded his refinery operations, keeping tight control of expenses and avoiding speculation. These practices inspired confidence on the part of Cleveland's bankers, and they provided him with ample financing.

There is no question that Rockefeller was a tough competitor who took advantage of every edge available to him. This is not surprising, however, considering the way he was raised. His father used to trade with John D. and his brothers and cheat them in the process in order to, as he said, "make 'em sharp."

One edge that Rockefeller ruthlessly exploited was secrecy. By guaranteeing to ship large quantities, he obtained secret rebates from the railroads. With this cost advantage, he was able to undercut the prices of competing refineries, and they were driven to the point of bankruptcy. Rockefeller would then acquire the refineries for cash or stock. Often, however, he was able to keep the acquisition secret, and his other competitors frequently did not know that supposedly independent firms were actually controlled by Rockefeller.

By 1880, companies controlled by Rockefeller refined 95 percent of the oil produced in the United States. Using first a trust and then later a holding company, Rockefeller was able to keep his oil monopoly intact. But in 1911, the U.S. Supreme Court finally ended it. The dissolution left Standard Oil of New Jersey, the holding company, with three large refineries on the East Coast, most of the overseas business, a lot of money, but very little crude oil. Then in 1921, it organized Standard Oil of Venezuela, which later became Creole Petroleum. It also obtained substantial crude from its Canadian subsidiary, Imperial Oil Ltd.

In 1948, Exxon acquired a 30 percent interest in the Arabian American Oil Company, which gave it access to an enormous supply of Saudi Arabian crude oil. Since then, the company has had an adequate supply of oil.

CHAPTER 17
INCO LIMITED

RETURN ON BOOK VALUE	PAYOUT RATIO	PRICE/EARNINGS RATIO
71–80 High: 24.6%	71–80 High: 101%	71–80 High: 37
71–80 Low: 3.8%	71–80 Low: 27%	71–80 Low: 7
Assumed: 12.5%	Assumed: 45%	Assumed: 14

1981 Beginning Book Value per Share: $23.57

"IF YOU THINK there's a war coming, buy International Nickel stock." That was a rule that a shrewd investor once followed with success. To understand why this rule was successful, it is necessary to review the history of the company.

Inco Limited or International Nickel Company, as it was previously called, can trace its origins to the founding of Orford Copper in New Jersey in 1877 and Canadian Copper in Sudbury, Ontario, in 1886. These two companies were the major suppliers of nickel in North America. Most of their output went to the steel industry.

Wishing to ensure a friendly source of nickel for their U.S. Steel Company, the Morgan interests purchased Canadian Copper, Orford, and several smaller nickel companies in 1902. They also purchased additional mining rights to areas around the two largest known nickel deposits in the world—one in Sudbury, Ontario, and one in New Caledonia. The resulting combination, the International Nickel Company, controlled well over 90 percent of the world's nickel supply.

The reason International Nickel was such a good investment in wartime was that nickel is used in large quantities to make the

159

hardened steel necessary for armaments. And since International Nickel had a virtual monopoly on nickel production, it made substantial profits during armed conflicts.

World War I proved to be a bonanza for the company, as the demand for nickel steel in armaments became enormous. World War II, the Korean War, and the Vietnam War also produced surges in the demand for nickel steel, and Inco benefited accordingly.

To maintain its monopoly position in nickel, the company in 1928, on the advice of its lawyers, shifted its home base to Canada to avoid the American antitrust laws. If it had remained headquartered in the United States, its monopoly in nickel would undoubtedly have been broken up.

Until the Sixties, International Nickel continued to control the nickel market with at least a 90 percent share. But then the company became a victim of its own success. For many years, it had aggressively developed new uses for nickel which had boosted demand for the metal. As planned, this increased demand led to high profits for the company, but the high profits also attracted aggressive competitors. Inco was slow to react to the competition, and its share of the nickel market has dropped to 30 percent. This drop in market share plus poor demand in the steel industry have led to hard times for Inco.

In 1974, Inco attempted to diversify with the acquisition of ESB Ray-O-Vac Corporation, a battery manufacturer, but the results have been disappointing.

Inco's experiment with venture capital has been more successful. In 1975, it started a program to invest in emerging technologies that have the potential for rapid growth. One of its more promising investments is a 24 percent interest in Biogen, a European-based genetic engineering firm. Biogen was the first company using genetic engineering techniques to produce interferon, the anti-cancer substance. Biogen is also working to develop bacteria that could remove metals directly from ores in the ground. Such a breakthrough would have enormous implications for the mining industry.

Another promising investment is LIC Industries. LIC has developed a process using a laser to break the bond between sulfur and oxygen. The process has great promise as a means of controlling sulfur dioxide emissions from smelter plants.

In its own corporate laboratories, Inco is working to develop a nickel battery for use in electric vehicles. It has also created several new alloys that show substantial promise.

Based upon the method outlined in Chapter 1 of Part II, we project that Inco stock will rise in price from $16 to $70 a share by the end of the decade—an increase of 338 percent. The sharp-eyed reader will note that we have assumed a Price/Earnings Ratio of 14, which is not halfway between the historical high of 37 and the low of 7. We have done this to compensate for the fact that the high of 37 was abnormal, being produced in a year of very low earnings.

CHAPTER 18
SEARS, ROEBUCK & CO.

RETURN ON BOOK VALUE	PAYOUT RATIO	PRICE/EARNINGS RATIO
71–80 High: 15.0%	71–80 High: 71%	71–80 High: 30
71–80 Low: 8.2%	71–80 Low: 37%	71–80 Low: 7
Assumed: 12.0%	Assumed: 45%	Assumed: 18.5

1981 Beginning Book Value per Share: $24.38

O VER THE YEARS Sears has received thousands of letters from catalog customers. Following is one of the more amusing: "Gentlemen: The canned salmon you sent me in my last order was no good. It made my wife deathly sick. Please send me another lot; my mother-in-law is here this month."

Richard Sears was the stationmaster in a small town in Minnesota, in 1886, when a local jeweler refused to accept a shipment of watches. Seeing an opportunity, Sears contacted the watch manufacturer and received permission to sell the watches himself. The ease with which he was able to sell them persuaded him to go into the watch business. After moving to Chicago, which was a better distribution center, Sears hired Alvah Curtis Roebuck to service the watches being returned for adjustment and repair. Sears sold this business and moved to Iowa but then returned to Chicago a few years later to again team up with Roebuck selling watches.

The Sears, Roebuck catalog evolved from a watch publication Sears put together listing some twenty-five items. By 1893, it consisted of sixty-four pages, advertising a wide range of articles from guns to baby carriages. It grew in a few years to over a thousand pages, becoming known as the "farmer's Bible."

The success of the Sears, Roebuck catalog was directly attributable to the promotional genius of Richard Sears. Mail-order firms until Sears had had only limited success. They had been unable to overcome the doubts of farmers, who were used to face-to-face dealing. While other mail-order firms such as Montgomery Ward required a money deposit along with each order, Sears instituted the policy of dispensing with deposits. In each Sears, Roebuck ad the words "Send No Money" were prominently displayed. He also emphasized in his ads that the customer was always right. If a customer was dissatisfied, he had his choice of either a new article or his money refunded.

These practices gained the trust of customers, and business expanded rapidly. Sears helped the expansion along with a promotional practice known as "Iowazation." Good customers throughout Iowa were selected to distribute Sears, Roebuck catalogs. If the customer agreed, Sears, Roebuck would ship twenty-four catalogs which the customer could then distribute among his friends and neighbors. Based upon the amount of orders the new catalog holder placed, the distributor received a valuable premium. Even if no orders came in, the distributor received a gift. When utilized nationally, this practice more than doubled the circulation of the catalog within a year.

Sears's enthusiasm for making sales frequently caused him to advertise items he didn't have. Being an optimist, he assumed that he could always get them later when the orders came in. Often there were great delays in filling orders. One customer wrote: "We are waiting for the special $5.95 baby buggy we ordered for our little son. Better change the order to a single-barrel shotgun and a plug of chewing tobacco. The kid is growing up."

Roebuck found many of Sears's business practices, such as advertising items not in stock, distasteful. In 1895, he sold his interest in the company to Sears for $25,000. Later Roebuck lost all of his money in Florida real estate, and he returned to the company as a clerk in 1933.

While advertising items not in stock was one of the reasons he lost his partner, Roebuck, it also gained Richard Sears a new one. Julius Rosenwald was a manufacturer of men's suits in Chicago. Sears appeared at Rosenwald's factory one day and asked to see some suits. After glancing at a few, Sears ordered fifty of them. He explained that he had already sold them and that he would be back for more as he received orders. Rosenwald was impressed and shortly thereafter purchased a sizable interest in Sears, Roebuck. He then began to take an active part in its management. Rosenwald proved his managerial competence by stabilizing the company's finances and bringing order to the formerly chaotic warehousing and order-filling process. In 1908, Sears resigned from the firm in a policy dispute, and Rosenwald assumed sole command.

In 1925, the company opened its first retail store under the direction of General Robert E. Wood. Under Wood's guidance, Sears was transformed from a mail-order firm into America's largest retailer. Wood was also responsible for the formation of Allstate Insurance.

In recent years Sears has fallen on hard times. In a misguided effort to woo more affluent customers in the late Sixties, Sears stocked more expensive, high-fashion merchandise, which only alienated its middle-income customers and drove them to discount chains. Then in a series of "quick fix" attempts, it rapidly adopted and abandoned discounting and specialty retailing in its stores. Now Sears has apparently recognized that it has to concentrate on what it did best—providing quality goods to middle-income families at reasonable prices and backing those goods with reliable service and meaningful guarantees of satisfaction. Executing this strategy is going to be difficult and will take patience, but we believe that if the company disdains "quick fixes" it can rebuild a reasonably profitable merchandising group. In the face of heightened competition from discount stores and shopping centers, Sears will never, we believe, regain its former dominance in retailing, but even average profitability will be acceptable in view of Sears's other strengths.

The real opportunity for Sears in the Eighties is in the area of financial services. With its huge customer base (over sixty million Americans have Sears charge cards), with its nationwide store locations, and with its enormous financial strength, Sears is in a position to garner large profits on financial service products. Already its Allstate Insurance subsidiary is contributing over 50 percent of the company's profits. Sears is in a position to further penetrate the personal insurance market. It also may evolve into banking services as legal restrictions diminish. Its recently announced formation of a money market fund seems to be a step in this direction.

Sears also has a major opportunity in the development and financing of real estate projects. Its Homart Development Company is the nation's third-largest developer of shopping centers.

In recognition of the enhanced prospects for growth that Sears has in financial services and real estate, the company has recently restructured its management to allow it to better exploit opportunities in these areas. We view these changes as positive developments.

Based upon the method outlined in Chapter 1 of Part II, we project that Sears stock will rise in price from $17 to $90 a share by the end of the decade—an increase of 429 percent.

CHAPTER 19
STANDARD OIL OF CALIFORNIA

RETURN ON BOOK VALUE	PAYOUT RATIO	PRICE/EARNINGS RATIO
71–80 High: 25.9%	71–80 High: 46%	71–80 High: 13
71–80 Low: 11.1%	71–80 Low: 26%	71–80 Low: 4
Assumed: 15.0%	Assumed: 40%	Assumed: 8.5

1981 Beginning Book Value per Share: $32.38

ASED UPON THE method outlined in Chapter 1 of Part II, we project that Standard Oil of California stock will rise in price from $39 to $82 a share by the end of the decade —an increase of 110 percent.

Unlike Texaco, its Aramco partner, Standard Oil of California (Socal) reacted quickly to the jump in world oil prices in the early Seventies. It rapidly developed an aggressive oil exploration program seeking domestic U.S. sources. Using advanced seismic data-processing techniques, the company has made major finds in the Rocky Mountains, Alaska, and the southeastern United States. Its domestic exploration results have been rated as outstanding by many analysts.

The company has also positioned itself to participate in synthetic fuels. Socal is the largest holder of privately owned oil-shale lands in the United States. It is building a shale-oil plant in Utah that should begin production in 1983. The company has also been active in geothermal exploration.

Socal owns a 20 percent interest in Amax Inc., the giant U.S. metals and mining concern. It is likely that it will acquire the remaining 80 percent at some point in the future. Such an acquisition would give Socal a better geographic balance, since 70 percent of Amax's assets are in the United States. With access to Socal's ample cash flow, Amax's resource base in coal, molybdenum, and other metals could be more aggressively developed.

In recognition of Socal's great progress during the Seventies, its chairman was recently selected by a major Wall Street publication as the best chief executive officer in the international oil industry.

Standard Oil Company of California began as a part of John D. Rockefeller's original Standard Oil Company. Rockefeller had established a San Francisco branch office for his company and was sending oil to California from Pennsylvania in clipper ships by way of Cape Horn. The California producers resisted Rockefeller's invasion, but the discovery of a huge oilfield in Los Angeles doomed them. Overproduction led to collapsing oil prices and financial chaos. Rockefeller stepped in and bought up a major independent producer at bargain prices, making his the dominant oil company on the Pacific Coast.

By the time of the dissolution of Standard Oil by the Supreme Court, in 1911, Socal was a fully integrated oil company possessing its own refineries, oil wells, and marketing outlets. By 1919, the company was producing 26 percent of the total U.S. oil production.

Socal's great stroke of luck occurred in the Thirties. Shortly before World War I, British Petroleum, Shell, the French government, and seven American oil companies, including Exxon, Mobil, and later Gulf, had joined together to form the Turkish Petroleum Company for the purpose of exploring for oil in Iraq. In forming the company, the partners agreed that all oil exploration in the Middle East would be conducted through Turkish Petroleum. They wouldn't explore individually.

In the late Twenties, Exxon and Gulf were both offered an oil concession in Bahrain, in the Persian Gulf. They both turned it down because of their Turkish Petroleum agreement. Gulf, however, interested Socal in the concession, and Socal purchased it. Socal was not a partner in Turkish Petroleum and thus was not bound by the joint exploration agreement. In 1931, Socal struck oil in Bahrain. Bahrain never became a major oil producer, but

Socal's experience there suggested that major oil deposits existed on the Saudi Arabian mainland twenty miles away.

Meanwhile, King Ibn Saud of Saudi Arabia was searching for new sources of revenue. The king's advisers suggested that money could be raised by selling oil exploration rights. They approached Texaco, Exxon, and Gulf, which turned down the proposition. Socal, however, learned of the offer and swiftly agreed to purchase it. From their Bahrain experience, Socal's managers knew of Saudi Arabia's potential. So, for $150,000 in gold, plus a $100,000 gold loan and $25,000 a year rent in gold, Socal purchased what has turned out to be the single most valuable asset on earth—the Saudi Arabian oilfields.

Socal soon realized the extent of its bonanza and in 1936 decided to take in Texaco as a partner. Texaco was the only other major American oil company not bound by the Turkish Petroleum agreement. Texaco gave Socal access to new markets and additional capital. A jointly owned company, Caltex, was established to manage their combined operation.

After World War II, the Saudi Arabian bonanza became too big for Socal and Texaco to handle alone. Thus, they offered Exxon and Mobil each 20 percent of their interest. Mobil had doubts about the potential of Saudi Arabia and took only a 10 percent share. Exxon snapped up its own share plus the 10 percent Mobil didn't take. Thus, Texaco, Socal, and Exxon became equal partners in Aramco—Arabian American Oil Company. The total cost to Exxon and Mobil of purchasing their interests was about $500 million.

CHAPTER 20
WESTINGHOUSE

RETURN ON BOOK VALUE	PAYOUT RATIO	PRICE/EARNINGS RATIO
71–80 High: 18.4%	71–80 High: 61%	71–80 High: 26
71–80 Low: 1.5%	71–80 Low: 25%	71–80 Low: 4
Assumed: 14.0%	Assumed: 40%	Assumed: 15

1981 Beginning Book Value per Share: $29.81

BASED UPON THE method outlined in Chapter 1 of Part II, we project that Westinghouse stock will rise in price from $27 to $119 a share by the end of the decade—an increase of 341 percent.

The Westinghouse Company was formed in 1866 by George Westinghouse to manufacture and promote the use of alternating-current (AC) electrical equipment. At the time, the fundamental problem of the infant electric industry was how to transmit power over substantial distances. The direct-current (DC) generators of the day could not provide electricity economically at a distance of more than a mile from the generation site.

Westinghouse had learned that a French and English engineer had invented a rudimentary system of distributing alternating current. Recognizing the potential, he acquired the patent rights and directed his engineering staff to improve the system and design equipment to be used with it. The key to the success of alternating current (AC) was that its voltage (pressure) could be increased greatly, allowing for transmission over long distances. The voltage could then be reduced to a manageable level when the electricity had reached its point of use.

Alternating current was not without its opponents. Thomas

169

Edison still advocated direct current, believing that its limitations could ultimately be overcome. Others emphasized that direct current was safe compared to the dangerously high voltages involved in alternating current. To prove how dangerous alternating current was, one opponent actually purchased Westinghouse equipment through middlemen and installed it in a prison—creating the first electric chair.

Westinghouse, however, convinced the public that alternating current was safe when he illuminated the entire 1893 Columbian Exhibition in Chicago using his system. Shortly thereafter, the Westinghouse Company won the contract to install three large alternating-current generators at Niagara Falls, creating the nation's first large hydroelectric project. The Niagara generators were a huge success, and alternating current became the standard for the electric utility industry.

Having revolutionized the electric utility industry once, it was natural that Westinghouse should participate in the second great revolution—nuclear power. In 1957, Westinghouse built the first commercial atomic power plant. It thereafter committed a large portion of its resources to developing nuclear power technology.

In the face of stiff competition from other nuclear plant manufacturers, Westinghouse hit upon a way to sell its nuclear plants to utilities. It would guarantee to sell uranium fuel to the utilities at a very favorable price if they purchased a Westinghouse plant. This was an excellent sales technique, and many utilities ordered Westinghouse plants as a consequence. The scheme, however, had one flaw. Westinghouse didn't have enough uranium to meet its contractual commitments. It was counting on buying the uranium in the open market. Unfortunately for Westinghouse, uranium prices skyrocketed, and by 1974, the company notified its utility customers that it would be unable to supply uranium at the agreed price. Huge lawsuits were filed, and Westinghouse was in a precarious situation.

Fortunately for Westinghouse shareholders, these lawsuits have now been settled, and a great cloud has been lifted from the company. The lawsuits, however, prevented the company for several years from concentrating on opportunities for the future.

Apparently to make up for lost time, Westinghouse has recently purchased Teleprompter, the nation's largest cable TV operator. The acquisition makes a great deal of sense, since Westinghouse already has a successful group of TV stations, and cable will provide an additional outlet for its programming. Westinghouse will also be able to provide the capital and good reputation necessary to win additional cable franchises. The only reservation is the enormous price tag. Teleprompter will have to be exceptionally profitable to justify the price Westinghouse paid.

Westinghouse has a strong position in defense-related products and should benefit significantly from increased military spending. It is also aggressively implementing Japanese-style management techniques in an attempt to boost productivity and quality. The results of this attempt are being closely followed by other American corporations.

CHAPTER 21
UNION CARBIDE

RETURN ON BOOK VALUE	PAYOUT RATIO	PRICE/EARNINGS RATIO
71–80 High: 25.3%	71–80 High: 79%	71–80 High: 20
71–80 Low: 8.6%	71–80 Low: 31%	71–80 Low: 4
Assumed: 13.0%	Assumed: 50%	Assumed: 12

1981 Beginning Book Value per Share: $70.89

ESPITE BEING ONE of America's largest corporations, Union Carbide is not well known by the public. The reason is that the company sells primarily to other companies rather than directly to consumers. Even those items sold directly to the public, such as Eveready batteries, Prestone antifreeze, and Glad plastic bags, are not associated by consumers with Union Carbide.

In recent years, the company has undergone a major restructuring to emphasize those businesses in which it has a leading position. Marginal businesses have been sold off or liquidated. The result is a company that has substantial growth potential.

Union Carbide is a major producer of gases such as nitrogen and oxygen. Despite being mundane products, they have very exciting outlooks. Nitrogen is being used in increasing quantities by the petroleum industry to stimulate oil-well production. Oxygen has a bright future in the synthetic-fuels industry. Most coal gasification technologies require large amounts of oxygen, and this could develop into a huge new market.

Another area that has significant potential for Union Carbide is carbon. The company is the world's leading producer of graphite electrodes, which are used in electric arc furnaces. The electric arc method of making steel is rapidly growing. High-performance carbon fibers are also becoming a significant area. They are being used increasingly in the aerospace industry, where high strength-to-weight ratios are important. They are also used in golf clubs and tennis rackets.

Batteries should provide another area of growth in the Eighties. More and more devices are being introduced that are powered by batteries. Under the Eveready name, the company has recently introduced a new line of lithium batteries.

Despite its potential, however, Union Carbide is not without problems. Perhaps the major obstacle it faces in the Eighties is maintaining its basic petrochemical business in the face of competition from new plants being built in OPEC countries. These plants will enjoy substantial advantages in raw-material costs, since they are located next to oil and gas fields. Union Carbide has attempted to minimize the effect of this new competition by licensing its own proprietary technology for use in building the plants. By doing so, Union Carbide will receive royalties off the total production of the OPEC plants.

Based upon the method outlined in Chapter 1 of Part II, we project that Union Carbide stock will rise in price from $49 to $183 a share by the end of the decade—an increase of 273 percent.

The Union Carbide and Carbon Company was formed in 1917 out of a merger of four companies: the Prest-O-Lite Company, the Linde Air Products Company, the National Carbon Company, and the Union Carbide Company. The merger of these companies was a natural outgrowth of their common interest in acetylene, a colorless, highly flammable gas.

In 1892, in an attempt to make aluminum in an electric furnace, two experimenters produced calcium carbide and, from it, acetylene. In 1898, they interested a group of investors in forming the Union Carbide Company. The company was to manufacture carbide and thereby acetylene for street and home lighting.

To manufacture their carbide in an electric furnace, Union Carbide made use of carbon electrodes furnished by the National Carbon Company. National Carbon had produced the world's first commercial dry-cell battery, which it marketed under the Eveready trademark.

Meanwhile, scientists in France had discovered that an intense metal-cutting flame could be produced by burning acetylene in oxygen. Since there was no company manufacturing oxygen in the United States, several electrode makers pooled their resources and established the Linde Air Products Company.

In 1914, the Prest-O-Lite Company, which manufactured acetylene lamps for automobiles, began searching for a way to make synthetic acetylene. In the course of its investigation, it worked in close contact with the other companies involved with acetylene. Realizing their common interests, the four companies arranged a merger.

During World War I, the newly formed Union Carbide found itself with requests to make materials never before made in the United States—helium for dirigibles, ferrozirconium for armor-plating, and activated carbon for gas masks. Demonstrating the technical prowess that was to become a hallmark of the company, Union Carbide was able to fulfill the requests made of it.

In 1919, the company first produced synthetic ethylene. Forseeing the potential of synthetic organic chemicals, the company formed a chemical division, and America's petrochemical industry was born.

In 1926, the company acquired vanadium deposits on the Colorado Plateau. Vanadium is used to make steel alloys. From these deposits, uranium was produced, which, during World War II, led to the company's heavy involvement in atomic energy. In 1943, the company was selected to operate the Oak Ridge, Tennessee, facility which produced material for America's first atomic bomb. During the war, Union Carbide also perfected butadiene, which made America's wartime synthetic-rubber program successful.

After the war, Union Carbide became a major producer of polyethylene, the plastic used originally in "squeeze bottles" and then in sheeting and thin films for packaging. The company also supplied huge amounts of liquid oxygen, hydrogen, and nitrogen for America's space program.

So diversified is Union Carbide in basic materials that, at last count in 1976, it worked with 90 of the 107 chemical elements isolated and named by scientists.

CHAPTER 22
PROCTER & GAMBLE

RETURN ON BOOK VALUE	PAYOUT RATIO	PRICE/EARNINGS RATIO
71–80 High: 20.0%	71–80 High: 48%	71–80 High: 33
71–80 Low: 17.4%	71–80 Low: 42%	71–80 Low: 8
Assumed: 16.5%	Assumed: 45%	Assumed: 20.5

1981 Beginning Book Value per Share: $43.52

PROCTER & GAMBLE began in 1837 in "Porkopolis," when an English candlemaker and an Irish soapmaker formed a partnership. "Porkopolis," otherwise known as Cincinnati, Ohio, was an excellent location for their business, since the city was a large hog-butchering center. Animal fat was a key ingredient in both soap and candles.

The business of the two partners prospered. During the Civil War, Procter & Gamble became a major supplier to the Union Army. Unlike some unscrupulous manufacturers, James Gamble made certain that the company delivered full cases of first-quality candles and soap to the Union forces.

In 1879, the company produced its first major brand-name product—Ivory Soap. The soap had been invented by accident. A workman had left a machine operating with a large batch of soap in it while he went to lunch. When he returned, he found that air had been worked into the mixture. Rather than discard the batch, the company wrapped and sold it. A few weeks later, store owners downriver from Cincinnati began ordering more of "that soap that floats." It seems that their customers had found

175

that the floating soap solved the problem presented by a soap bar at the bottom of a bathtub or basin filled with brown river water. Upon discovering that the soap contained only .56 percent impurities, Harley Procter conceived of one of the most famous advertising phrases of all time—"$99^{44}/_{100}\%$ Pure." With Ivory Soap, Procter & Gamble began its long tradition of extensive consumer advertising.

Around the turn of the century, Procter & Gamble entered the cottonseed-oil business. It was a natural diversification, since large quantities of the oil were used in soap. Out of experiments with hydrogenation, the company in 1911 created a major new consumer product—Crisco. Crisco was the first hydrogenated all-vegetable shortening.

In 1932, Procter & Gamble sponsored the first daytime radio drama, *The Puddle Family*. This form of entertainment has been called a soap opera ever since in recognition of the fact that a soap company sponsored the first program. The company still sponsors *As the World Turns, Search for Tomorrow, The Guiding Light,* and *Another World* on daytime TV. These soap operas are direct descendants of *The Puddle Family*.

In 1946, Procter & Gamble revolutionized home laundering when it introduced Tide. Tide was the first synthetic chemical compound that actually pulled dirt out of fabrics and dissolved it in wash water. It eliminated much of the drudgery required to get clothes clean.

In the Fifties and Sixties, Procter & Gamble continued to diversify, acquiring Duncan Hines (1956), Charmin Paper Mills (1957), and Folger's (1963). The company also introduced a string of exceptionally successful products. Introduced in 1955, Crest garnered the lion's share of the toothpaste market after Procter & Gamble was able to persuade the American Dental Association to endorse it. Pampers, introduced a few years later, has gone on to be the company's single biggest revenue producer.

There is no secret to Procter & Gamble's success. Its formula is a very simple one: Develop a product that is superior in some significant way to anything on the market, manufacture that product to the highest standards of quality, and then extensively advertise the product to acquaint consumers with the product's superiority. The success that Procter & Gamble has had following this formula is unprecedented. The corporation is without question America's premier consumer goods company.

In spite of its tremendous overall success, Procter & Gamble has had its share of failures. Rely, its tampon product, has been the most spectacular. Pringles, the potato chip in a can, was another notable failure.

One recently introduced product that appears to have great potential is Attends. This is essentially an "adult Pampers" designed for use with incontinent adults. The potential market for this product is estimated to be $4 billion. Another impressive new product is High Point, a decaffeinated coffee which apparently has a significantly better flavor than Sanka. Procter & Gamble also appears ready to mount a major attack in the soft-drink industry. It recently acquired Crush orange drink. The company has been at work on a home-carbonated soft drink for several years. Procter & Gamble takes its research on new products very seriously. In 1980, it spent $227 million on research and development.

Procter & Gamble's corporate goal is to double its size each decade. It has consistently achieved this target in the past. Achieving it in the Eighties may prove somewhat more difficult in view of the company's present enormous size, but we are inclined to believe that their current management can accomplish this task.

Based upon the method outlined in Chapter 1 of Part II, we project that Procter & Gamble stock will rise in price from $68 to $295 a share by the end of the decade—an increase of 334 percent.

CHAPTER 23
UNITED
TECHNOLOGIES

RETURN ON BOOK VALUE	PAYOUT RATIO	PRICE/EARNINGS RATIO
71–80 High: 28.1%	71–80 High: 43%	71–80 High: 12
71–80 Low: Deficit	71–80 Low: Deficit	71–80 Low: Deficit
Assumed: 13.5%	Assumed: 40%	Assumed: 6

1981 Beginning Book Value per Share: $31.29

NITED AIRCRAFT AND Transport, the forerunner of United Technologies, almost became the "General Motors of the Air." By 1929, it owned aircraft manufacturers Vought, Boeing, and Sikorsky, engine manufacturer Pratt & Whitney, five airlines that ultimately became United Airlines, and several suppliers of aircraft components. However, the company was split up in 1934, when a federal law was passed prohibiting airlines associated with aircraft manufacturers from being awarded air mail contracts. Three separate companies emerged from the split-up—Boeing, United Airlines, and United Aircraft.

As a separate company, United Aircraft remained a major supplier of engines and parts to the airplane industry. During World War II, the company devoted itself to the United States war effort. Its Pratt & Whitney subsidiary and its licensees produced half of all the horsepower used by American air forces during the war.

After the war, United Aircraft became the dominant manufacturer of jet engines. At times it almost had a monopoly on their production. General Electric and Rolls-Royce, however, developed into potent competitors, and the companies have since engaged in epic struggles for the lucrative market.

Overly dependent on the boom-and-bust aerospace industry, United Aircraft in 1971 recruited a Litton Industries executive to oversee a diversification of the company's business. The directors believed that the company needed other sources of income to underwrite engine research during lean periods in aerospace.

Under Harry Gray, United Aircraft purchased Otis Elevator, Carrier Corporation (air conditioning), Essex International (controls), Ambac Industries (diesel fuel injectors), and Mostek (semiconductors). To reflect the addition of these businesses, the name of the company was changed to United Technologies.

The theory underlying these acquisitions is that they all have the ability to benefit from the enormous amount of research that the company performs in its basic aerospace business. Otis Elevator, for example, has recently begun selling a fully electronic elevator control system that uses principles developed in avionic controls. The system cuts energy consumption by 40 percent.

In an attempt to become a "General Motors of Technology," the company is spending an enormous amount on research and development. It is among the top six companies in America in terms of the amount spent on R&D. No other major company spends more as a percentage of sales.

The company unquestionably has a bright future, but there are potential problems. In an effort to win engine contracts on Boeing's new 757 airplane, United Technologies has apparently given some potentially expensive guarantees to certain airlines. If its engine fails to use 8 percent less fuel than an equivalent Rolls-Royce engine, United Technologies apparently has agreed to make up the difference in fuel costs to the airlines for ten years. This could amount to large sums of money. The gamble, however, is probably worth it in view of the lucrative jet engine market. A jet engine is in a way similar to a razor. More money can be made in supplying the spare parts than in making the original machine.

Based upon the method outlined in Chapter 1 of Part II, we project that United Technologies stock will rise in price from $43 to $47 a share by the end of the decade—an increase of 9 percent.

This relatively low forecast comes from the fact that United Technologies has had a very low Price/Earnings Ratio for the entire decade of the Seventies. The result is that under our projection method we were forced to assign it a Price/Earnings Multiple of 6. If United Technologies' research and development programs pay off as expected, however, the company could easily have a Price/Earnings Ratio of 16 by the end of the decade. That would translate into a price of $126. For the sake of consistency, however, we are forced to use the lower price as our official projection in spite of the fact that we believe that it will be on the low side.

CHAPTER 24
OWENS-ILLINOIS

RETURN ON **BOOK VALUE**	**PAYOUT RATIO**	**PRICE/EARNINGS** **RATIO**
71–80 High: 12.8%	71–80 High: 37%	71–80 High: 18
71–80 Low: 9.4%	71–80 Low: 27%	71–80 Low: 4
Assumed: 11.0%	Assumed: 40%	Assumed: 11

1981 Beginning Book Value per Share: $43.56

‖T IS HARD to conceive, but until 1903, all glass bottles in the world were blown by hand. Milk bottles, beer bottles, medicine bottles, and all the thousands of other kinds of bottles were produced one at a time by glassblowers. The thirty or forty thousand glassblowers in the United States were highly unionized in 1900. They made a very high wage compared to other workers, $15 to $20 a day. But theirs was a very unhealthy occupation with a short life expectancy. Few glassblowers escaped without lung or facial problems.

Michael Owens was a glassblower in the bottle factory owned by Edward Libbey. He did not wish to die young. After much tinkering, Owens invented a machine that could produce bottles in 1897. By 1903, the machine was perfected, and Owens, along with his former employer, Edward Libbey, formed the Owens Bottle Machine Company.

The machine revolutionized the glass bottle industry over the next fifteen years. The glassblowers, however, did not thank Owens for inventing his machine, which undoubtedly saved many men from premature death. The glassblowers' union reacted with strikes and work stoppages, but they could not stop the introduction of the new bottle machines. Ironically, Owens had initially offered to sell the patents for his machine to the union. The union, however, refused to believe that the machine would ever work.

Since there was no dominant bottle company at the time, Owens's company licensed his machine to several different companies each specializing in a different type of bottle—milk bottles, beer bottles, etc. One of the licensees was the Illinois Glass Works, which had the rights to use the machine to make liquor and medicine bottles. Not content with just licensing, the Owens company later itself expanded into manufacturing beer bottles and narrow-necked food bottles such as those used for catsup.

Owens's company was in a position to gain control of the entire glass bottle industry through either licensing or direct production when a young MIT graduate invented a machine sufficiently different from Owens's to avoid patent problems. The rest of the industry adopted this machine, and the Owens company lost its chance for total control.

In 1929, the Owens company merged with its licensee, Illinois Glass Works, to become Owens-Illinois Glass Company. The company almost merged with Continental Can, but the 1929 crash caused the merger plan to be dropped. In 1935, the company acquired the Libbey Glass Company. This was the same company that Michael Owens had worked for when he invented his bottle machine. In 1968, Owens-Illinois merged with Lily Tulip Cup Company, which gave it a substantial position in wood-based packaging.

Today Owens-Illinois is the dominant factor in the bottle business and a major factor in other forms of packaging. Unfortunately, these areas are basically mature industries which should grow only as fast as the general economy. Certain segments such as plastic bottles promise to grow rapidly, but this growth will come at the expense of the other segments such as glass bottles.

Until recently, Owens-Illinois tried to be all things to all customers. If a customer wanted a distinctive bottle, Owens-Illinois would make it for him in spite of the low profit that the order would generate. As a consequence, Owens-Illinois has had a Return on Book Value far below American industry as a whole. Now Owens-Illinois has come to the realization that profits are more important than volume, and the company is rigorously pruning marginal products.

Executives at Owens-Illinois, like executives at many other American companies, have been volume-oriented. That is, they have made new investments with the idea of expanding production so that they can sell more of their product. While this tactic can build sales, more often it simply leads to reduced profitability. The reason is that the competition is usually following the same strategy. The result is that the industry suffers from substantial overcapacity and low profits. For many years, the packaging industry has followed this scenario, and its profitability has been substantially below average.

Now Owens-Illinois is being managed with the goal of increasing profitability. To achieve this result, it is closing high-cost plants and pruning low-profit products. Recently Owens-Illinois closed a six-year-old plant in New England. This was the first time that the company had closed a plant since World War II. The move took courage but it showed the resolve that current management is bringing to its task.

At some point in the future, Owens-Illinois may, like American Can, decide to sell off its wood-products division. The division owns 1.1 million acres of valuable timberland. Such a sale might bring the company as much cash per share as the shares are currently selling for on the open market ($26).

Based upon the method outlined in Chapter 1 of Part II, we project that Owens-Illinois stock will rise in price from $26 to $88 a share by the end of the decade—an increase of 238 percent.

CHAPTER 25
ALLIED
CORPORATION

RETURN ON BOOK VALUE	PAYOUT RATIO	PRICE/EARNINGS RATIO
71–80 High: 19.9%	71–80 High: 64%	71–80 High: 18
71–80 Low: 7.6%	71–80 Low: 27%	71–80 Low: 5
Assumed: 14.0%	Assumed: 45%	Assumed: 11.5

1981 Beginning Book Value per Share: $47.48

THE WASHINGTON POST and Allied Corporation (formerly Allied Chemical Company) would not appear to have anything in common. Yet both were controlled by the same man, Eugene Meyer.

Meyer, a Wall Street financier, purchased the *Washington Post* for $825,000 at an auction in 1933. He had previously offered $5 million for the paper in 1929 but was turned down. The paper is controlled today by his daughter, Kathryn Meyer Graham.

Meyer's involvement with Allied Chemical extends to an earlier date. Meyer had served in various government posts as a dollar-a-year man during World War I. He had seen at close hand the wartime shortages that occurred in dyes, pharmaceuticals, and other necessities when imports from Germany ceased. Shortly after the war, Meyer lent his support to a consolidation of five existing American chemical companies to create a firm that could compete with the Germans. The result was Allied Chemical and Dye. Meyer became a major stockholder in the company.

One of Allied's first projects was the establishment of a plant

184

in 1921 to obtain nitrogen from the air. Nitrogen is a crucial ingredient in explosives and in fertilizer. Just before World War I, a German company developed a process which would take nitrogen out of the air and form ammonia (ammonia being one part nitrogen to three parts hydrogen). Allied was the first American chemical company to duplicate the process commercially.

In subsequent years, Allied expanded its chemical businesses. In 1962, it bought a petroleum company to provide it with raw materials for its extensive chemical operations. In the late Sixties, the company made the decision to expand further into oil and gas—not as a source of raw materials but strictly as an investment. The company was concerned about the lackluster growth prospects of its chemical businesses and wanted to diversify into another area.

Through the purchase of properties in the North Sea and Indonesia, Allied's diversification was a huge success as the price of oil skyrocketed in the Seventies. In 1980, 80 percent of the company's profits came from oil and gas.

The success of its oil and gas business, however, obscured fundamental problems with many of Allied's other businesses. In 1979, the board of directors hired a United Technologies executive to restructure the company. He has since sold off several of the company's unprofitable businesses and trimmed sharply the company's executive ranks. He has also engineered the acquisition of Eltra and Bunker-Ramo.

The key question concerning Allied Corp.'s future is how well it can invest the cash being generated by its oil properties. So far it is off to a good start, but the ultimate success of its program remains to be seen.

Based upon the method outlined in Chapter 1 of Part II, we project that Allied Corp.'s stock will rise in price from $45 to $138 a share by the end of the decade—an increase of 207 percent.

CHAPTER 26
JOHNS-MANVILLE

RETURN ON
BOOK VALUE
71–80 High: 16.3%
71–80 Low: 6.1%
Assumed: 10.5%

PAYOUT RATIO
71–80 High: 78%
71–80 Low: 32%
Assumed: 50%

PRICE/EARNINGS
RATIO
71–80 High: 19
71–80 Low: 4
Assumed: 11.5

1981 Beginning Book Value per Share: $40.29

JOHNS-MANVILLE IS A leading producer of fiberglass and other insulations. It is also, unfortunately, the world's largest manufacturer of asbestos products.

Asbestos is a fibrous mineral that has very unusual properties. It is fireproof and heat-resistant while being very workable. It is used in over three thousand products for which acceptable substitutes do not exist. Asbestos is used in clutch facings and brake linings for airplanes and automobiles as well as insulation for steam pipes, boilers, and nuclear reactors.

In solid form, asbestos is perfectly safe. However, it has been discovered that asbestos dust can cause cancer and other serious lung diseases. The problem is that asbestos dust particles are very sharp and are so fine that when they are inhaled, neither the nasal hairs nor the mucous membrane in the nose catch them. The result is that they reach the lungs quite readily. Once in the lungs, they remain there. They are not exhaled. Acting as irritants, they can produce difficulty in breathing and, frequently, lung cancer. These problems, however, can take many years to manifest themselves.

Workers in shipyards during World War II were exposed to high levels of asbestos dust, as have been workers in other industries. It is estimated that as many as eight million workers have been exposed to asbestos dust, but it is not known how many have inhaled dangerous levels. However, some of the workers that have developed asbestos-related diseases are now suing asbestos producers and other companies to recover damages for the injuries they have suffered. Johns-Manville, as the leading producer of asbestos, is a main target of these lawsuits.

Currently Johns-Manville is the defendant or co-defendant in over five thousand asbestos-related health suits. It is unknown how many remain to be filed. Johns-Manville is apparently protected by liability insurance against most of these claims. Its insurance, however, will not protect the company against claims for punitive damages.

When a person is injured by the wrongful act of another, the courts allow him to sue the responsible party for compensatory damages. Compensatory damages are that sum of money that will reimburse the injured party for his medical expenses, lost income, and pain and suffering. The amount of money awarded is at least theoretically related to the extent of the injury actually suffered. Some states, however, allow juries to award a plaintiff punitive damages in addition to compensatory damages. Punitive damages are an award of money that is not intended to compensate the injured party but rather to punish the responsible person and thus deter future acts of wrongdoing. Punitive damages do not have to be related to the extent of the injury suffered. Thus a plaintiff can be awarded $1,000 in compensatory damages plus $1 million in punitive damages. Interestingly enough, the money awarded as punitive damages goes to the plaintiff and not to the state, in spite of the fact that punitive damages are not intended to compensate the victim for his injury. They are, in a way, "windfall profits."

From Johns-Manville's point of view, the crucial thing about punitive damages is that they are not covered by insurance. Thus if juries award sizable punitive damages in each of the existing five thousand suits, Johns-Manville could be in the position of having to come up with millions of dollars out of corporate funds. If the awards are large enough, they could eventually bankrupt the company. The unfortunate thing about this situation is that in recent years Johns-Manville has made extraordinary efforts to protect its workers and others against injury from asbestos but, under legal rules, it will not be able to introduce this evidence to defend against punitive damage claims.

In recognition of the fact that the system of individual lawsuits is not an effective method of dealing with the enormous problem of compensating asbestos-injured workers, Congress is likely to pass some sort of legislation setting benefit levels and procedures for recovery. That such a system can work was shown by the program developed to deal with the problem of black-lung disease among coal miners. Until such legislation passes, however, Johns-Manville's future is uncertain.

If the asbestos problem is resolved without serious financial harm to Johns-Manville, the company has a favorable outlook. Only about 6 percent of its sales come from asbestos fibers. The rest comes from forest products and insulation. With the increase in heating costs, insulation has become a growth business. In addition, sometime in the Eighties the housing market should revive, which would give the company's earnings an extra impetus.

Based upon the method outlined in Chapter 1 of Part II, we project that Johns-Manville stock will rise in price from $16 to $73 a share by the end of the decade—an increase of 356 percent. It should be emphasized that in this projection we are assuming that the asbestos problem will not financially harm the company. If this assumption proves untrue, then our projection will have to be radically altered downward.

Johns-Manville can trace its roots back to 1858, and the founding of the H. W. Johns Manufacturing Company of New York. Henry Johns had started the company to manufacture a roofing material made of felt and other substances waterproofed with pitch. Recognizing the need for fireproofing his roofing products, Johns became interested in asbestos, and in 1868 he received a patent on an asbestos compound that made roofing fire-resistant. Over the years, his company developed into a major supplier of asbestos products.

The western distributor for Johns's asbestos products was the Manville Covering Company of Milwaukee. In 1901, three years after Johns's death, the two companies merged, with Thomas Manville becoming president. To ensure access to asbestos, the company acquired the Jeffrey Mine in Quebec. The mine and its surrounding lands contain one of the world's largest deposits of asbestos.

In 1925, shortly after Manville's death, J. P. Morgan & Company purchased the company and distributed its stock to the public. The Morgan interests have remained a powerful influence in the company ever since.

Over the years, Johns-Manville acquired companies to broaden its line of insulation products. Since its asbestos products were effective only in temperatures between 32°F and 1,500°F, Johns-Manville acquired the Celite Company, a pioneer in high-temperature insulation, and the Banner Rock Wool Company, a leading producer of low-temperature and refrigeration insulations. In 1958, the company acquired L.O.F. Glass Fibers, a leading fiberglass insulation company. In 1979, the company acquired Olincraft, a major forest-products producer. The acquisition brought with it over 500,000 acres of timberland.

CHAPTER 27
AMERICAN BRANDS

RETURN ON BOOK VALUE	PAYOUT RATIO	PRICE/EARNINGS RATIO
71–80 High: 38.3%	71–80 High: 63%	71–80 High: 12
71–80 Low: 14.5%	71–80 Low: 38%	71–80 Low: 4
Assumed: 15.5%	Assumed: 50%	Assumed: 8

1981 Beginning Book Value per Share: $22.83

AMERICAN BRANDS, formerly known as American Tobacco, has suffered a tremendous decline in its share of the tobacco market. In 1911, it controlled almost 100 percent of the market. In the 1960s, it controlled approximately 25 percent. Today the company's share is estimated at 11 percent. Yet in spite of this dramatic decline, the company is earning more money today than ever before. The principal reason is that it has diversified out of tobacco to the point where 40 percent of its profits come from products such as Franklin Life Insurance, Master Locks, Sunshine Biscuits, Jim Beam Bourbon, and Jergen's Lotion.

Beginning in 1966, American Brands began taking the cash flow from its tobacco business and using it to buy up successful companies making consumer products. It acquired only companies that wished to be taken over. It has not engaged in hostile takeover attempts. The reason for this policy is that American Brands wants to retain the existing management in companies it acquires. It realizes that it is very difficult for outsiders to rebuild a management team in an already successful company.

The roots of American Brands can be traced to a farm in North Carolina. On returning to his farm near Durham after the Civil War, Washington Duke found that it had been looted by foraging troops. In one of the outbuildings, however, he discovered a quantity of Bright tobacco that had been overlooked by the looters. Duke sold some of this tobacco to carry him over the winter and planted the rest. Fortunately for him, a great demand emerged for Bright tobacco among former soldiers. They had become accustomed to chewing it during the Civil War and continued to demand it after returning to civilian life. Duke was able to build a thriving business selling Bright tobacco. However, his business came under severe pressure in the 1870s, when the Liggett & Myers Bull Durham brand ran away with the chewing-tobacco market.

James Duke, Washington's son, decided to avoid the competition of Liggett and Myers by shifting emphasis to cigarettes. At this time all cigarettes were rolled by hand. Duke had a great stroke of luck when his competitors all turned down a cigarette-rolling machine. Duke adopted the machine and made an agreement with its inventor which gave him a secret rebate if his competitors used the machine. The machine, after being refined, revolutionized the manufacture of cigarettes. It drove down the cost of manufacturing substantially and was ultimately employed by all companies. Subsequently, Duke began a price war, knowing that with the aid of his secret rebate he could outlast the competition. The result was that his competitors were driven to the wall, and they were combined into the American Tobacco Company, which Duke controlled.

Using his profits from cigarettes, Duke created a price war in chewing tobacco and acquired the other major companies as they were driven to the verge of bankruptcy. In this manner he acquired his old nemesis, Liggett & Myers, and the famous Bull Durham trade name. Duke had created a monopoly in the tobacco business.

Unfortunately for Duke, his activities had not gone unnoticed by the government, and in a 1911 antitrust suit the U.S. Supreme Court dissolved the company into Liggett & Myers, R. J. Reynolds, P. Lorillard, American Tobacco, and several smaller companies. Duke left the company and went on to organize Duke Power & Light. He also gave such a substantial sum of money to Trinity College in Durham, North Carolina, that the trustees changed its name to Duke University.

The company drifted for several years until George Washington Hill became president. Hill recognized the importance of mass advertising, and with the aid of advertising genius Albert Lasker he made Lucky Strike the best-selling cigarette brand in the country. Several years later one ad industry executive lamented that Hill wasn't around to combat the cancer stigma attached to cigarette smoking: "Hill would have made cancer fashionable."

In the early Fifties, American Brands was late in introducing filter-tip cigarettes, and it suffered a tremendous loss of market share as a consequence. This loss of share has continued to the present.

The one bright spot in American Brands' tobacco business is its ultra-low-tar cigarette Carlton. A study recently released by the government suggests that, statistically, smokers of ultra-low-tar cigarettes such as Carlton may not have mortality rates measurably different from those of nonsmokers. Studies such as this may prompt many smokers to shift to Carlton.

In the long run, however, it appears quite clear that the tobacco industry is due for further contraction. With a majority of the public believing that it is dangerous to be exposed to the fumes of a cigarette smoker, it is likely that further restrictions will be placed on smoking in public places. Increased health consciousness on the part of individuals should also lead to fewer smokers.

Based upon the method outlined in Chapter 1 of Part II, we project that American Brands stock will rise in price from $38 to $103 a share by the end of the decade—an increase of 171 percent.

CHAPTER 28
AMERICAN CAN

RETURN ON BOOK VALUE	PAYOUT RATIO	PRICE/EARNINGS RATIO
71–80 High: 14.9%	71–80 High: 83%	71–80 High: 17
71–80 Low: 6.6%	71–80 Low: 40%	71–80 Low: 4
Assumed: 11.0%	Assumed: 45%	Assumed: 10.5

1981 Beginning Book Value per Share: $50.89

WILLIAM "JUDGE" MOORE was a lawyer in Chicago around the turn of the century when he gave up the law for the more lucrative field of finance. With several associates, he organized within a short time the Diamond Match Company, the National Biscuit Company, the so-called Tin Plate Trust, and the American Can Company. The profits generated by these deals allowed him to wear the most expensive garment worn by a U.S. male up until that time, a $19,000 fur coat, and to operate a large stable of racehorses. Inflation has made $19,000 in Moore's day the equivalent of $190,000 today.

Despite his expensive habits, Moore was a shrewd deal maker. Sensing that the steel industry was ripe for either a war or a consolidation between Federal Steel (controlled by J. P. Morgan) and Carnegie Steel, Moore acquired every company that he could in the steel industry not allied with either the Morgan or Carnegie interests. He wound up with a group of companies that made 12 percent of the country's steel ingots and 90 percent of its tin plate. Tin plate, out of which tin cans are made, is essentially steel covered by a thin coating of tin. Using his domination of the tin plate industry, Moore then began acquiring every tin can manufacturer that he could. He ended up consolidating 90

193

percent of the U.S. can business into his American Can Company. Moore anticipated that this company would be included in any steel industry consolidation.

In 1901, when Morgan brought peace to the steel industry by acquiring Carnegie Steel, he also acquired Moore's Tin Plate Trust. Moore, however, exacted such stiff terms that Morgan was miffed and refused to acquire American Can for inclusion in the U.S. Steel Company. Thus American Can remained an independent company.

When Moore was merging the various can companies into American Can, he required that the sellers sign an agreement not to reenter the can business within three thousand miles of Chicago for fifteen years. Unfortunately, he apparently didn't require that the head of American Can sign the same pledge. A few years after the formation of the company, the man who actually had negotiated the various purchases left and formed Continental Can. Continental Can today is American Can's most formidable competitor.

In 1916, American Can avoided dissolution. While finding that the company had been formed in a blatant violation of the antitrust laws, the U.S. Supreme Court refused to break it up. The Court noted that American Can had not attempted to eliminate competition and that a decree would have been difficult to fashion in view of the small units that composed the company. None of the company's competitors had testified in favor of a breakup.

In subsequent years the company benefited from the American consumer's desire for convenience, and its sales expanded rapidly. An unusual source of business developed during Prohibition. Canadian distillers experimented with putting their liquor in cans because bootleggers couldn't duplicate the complicated process of multicolor lithographing on tin. In 1935, the company introduced one of the more abundant artifacts of our current civilization—the beer can. In 1957, American Can acquired the Dixie Cup Company and with it a substantial forest-products business.

In the Seventies, American Can began on what has turned out to be, for the most part, an unsuccessful diversification effort. On the advice of young business-school-trained "whiz kids," the company entered aluminum recycling and resource recovery. It also acquired record distribution companies and a direct-mail consumer marketing firm. Only the direct-mail firm has delivered respectable results. One of the record companies, Sam Goody Inc., was recently indicted for selling counterfeit records.

In an attempt to restructure the company to gain a higher return on assets, American Can has decided to sell its sizable forest-products division. The sale is expected to bring anywhere from $800 million to $1 billion. This amount compares to a total market value for the company's entire common stock of around $600 million.

This proposed sale highlights the enormous asset values behind many of the Dow companies. Assets representing only 20 percent of American Can's total holdings are worth more than the company's entire common stock.

American Can intends to use part of the proceeds from the proposed sale to strengthen its remaining businesses and to make a "significant acquisition" in an area compatible with its present operations. Some of the proceeds may also be used to repurchase shares in American Can.

Based upon the method outlined in Chapter 1 of Part II, we project that American Can stock will rise in price from $32 to $94 a share by the end of the decade—an increase of 194 percent.

CHAPTER 29
WOOLWORTH

RETURN ON BOOK VALUE	PAYOUT RATIO	PRICE/EARNINGS RATIO
71–80 High: 16.0%	71–80 High: 56%	71–80 High: 22
71–80 Low: 7.4%	71–80 Low: 27%	71–80 Low: 3
Assumed: 11.0%	Assumed: 40%	Assumed: 12.5

1981 Beginning Book Value per Share: $45.29

WHEN ONE THINKS of Woolworth, one immediately thinks of variety stores. Yet today the company consists of much more than just variety stores. Woolworth is a major factor in low-margin retailing through its Woolco discount stores. Its Kinney shoe division is a rapidly growing billion-dollar specialty retailer. And it is a major factor in retailing in Mexico, Canada, Great Britain, and Germany. U.S. variety stores account for only approximately one-quarter of the company's total sales.

Based upon the method outlined in Chapter 1 of Part II, we project that Woolworth stock will rise in price from $20 to $104 a share by the end of the decade—an increase of 420 percent.

For a man who would later become a merchant prince, Frank Woolworth had a particularly inauspicious start in retailing. On his first day as a clerk, the young "boob from the country," as Woolworth later described himself, bungled everything. Fortunately, his employer was understanding and gave Woolworth time to learn the correct procedures. While working as a clerk, Woolworth helped organize a 5-cent counter in the store to clear out surplus merchandise. The counter was such a success that

Woolworth conceived of starting a store that carried only 5-cent items.

With the help of his former employer, Woolworth opened "The Great Five Cent Store" in Utica, New York, in 1879. Because of its poor location, this store was not successful. Undaunted, Woolworth moved to Lancaster, Pennsylvania, which offered better prospects. Here his 5-cent store was a great success.

Woolworth's success was based on the concept that more money could be made in retailing by selling huge volumes of low-profit items than could be made by selling small amounts of big-profit items. He was one of the first mass merchandisers. To stimulate turnover, he had a single cash price and openly displayed his merchandise so that shoppers could browse. Up until this time, most storekeepers kept their wares out of the customer's reach.

While in Lancaster, Woolworth added 10-cent merchandise to broaden the range of goods he could offer. He kept the 5-cent merchandise on one side of the store and the 10-cent items on the other side. He changed the name of the store to Woolworth's 5 and 10 Cent Store to reflect the change.

Initially, Woolworth's sales weren't for 5- and 10-cent coins but for "shinplasters." Shinplasters were paper money in denominations of 3, 5, 10, 15, 25, and 50 cents that had been issued by Congress during the Civil War. They received their unusual name from Union soldiers who used them for bandages. They weren't redeemed until 1880.

In order to expand his business, Woolworth took in partners to open new stores. When his original employer's store failed, Woolworth, remembering his kindness, set him up with a fully stocked 5-and-10-cent store. Woolworth later changed this policy of taking in partners. From that point on, new stores were owned by Woolworth, while his managers shared in the profits. His original partners, however, continued to open more 5-and-10-cent stores on their own. In 1912, the former partners merged their chains into Woolworth's to create one gigantic chain.

In 1909, Woolworth took his ideas to England and started a chain of Three and Sixpence stores. He thus became one of America's first multinational businessmen. Threepence and sixpence were the closest things to 5 and 10 cents in English currency. Today, England has almost a thousand "Woolies."

By the Sixties, the variety-store concept of retailing had fully matured and faced intense competition. Supermarkets and drugstores had begun carrying many variety-store items. The Woolworth Company was slow to react to this change. However, Kresge, another variety-store chain, was not. It took Frank Woolworth's idea of accepting low-profit margins on a high volume of sales and turned it into the highly successful K-Mart discount chain. Belatedly, Woolworth followed Kresge into discounting, and its Woolco chain is the result.

Woolworth has never done as well as K-Mart in discount stores. Part of the reason is that Woolworth licensed many of the departments in its Woolco stores to outside suppliers. This lowered its expenses initially in opening the stores, but it has deprived the company of many high-profit lines. In recent years, Woolworth has bought back the licensed departments, and this augurs well for future profits.

A very successful recent innovation that has important implications for the future is Woolworth's new J. Brannam chain. "J. Brannam" stands for "Just Brand Names." The stores carry brand-name clothing at prices 20 to 60 percent below department and other specialty stores. Space in many Woolcos is being converted to J. Brannam, and sales apparently are exploding.

CHAPTER 30
AMERICAN TELEPHONE & TELEGRAPH

RETURN ON BOOK VALUE	PAYOUT RATIO	PRICE/EARNINGS RATIO
71–80 High: 13.4%	71–80 High: 65%	71–80 High: 14
71–80 Low: 9.0%	71–80 Low: 59%	71–80 Low: 5
Assumed: 13.5%	Assumed: 65%	Assumed: 9.5

1981 Beginning Book Value per Share: $65.51

A S MAIL SERVICE has deteriorated, the suggestion has been made that the U.S. Postal Service should be run by AT&T. The thought is that AT&T, which has run the bulk of the nation's phone systems so efficiently, might be able to rectify some of the problems at the post office.

Few people, however, are aware that for a year the Postal Service actually ran AT&T. During World War I, a movement to nationalize AT&T gained momentum, and in 1918 the government did nationalize it and placed it under the control of the Postal Service. The government controlled the telephone system for one year. During that time, rates were increased 20 percent, yet the company ran a $13 million deficit. In addition, shortly after assuming control the government instituted a connection charge for the installation of phones of new subscribers. Prior to its takeover, the government had repeatedly denied AT&T's request for such a charge. After its disastrous year of operating the phone system, the government turned it back to AT&T, but the connection charge still continues to this day.

The telephone itself was the result of an accident. In reading a copy in the original German of *On the Sensations of Tone*, by Hermann von Helmholtz, Alexander Graham Bell mistakenly understood that Helmholtz had sent spoken words via telegraph. Bell just tried to reconstruct what he thought Helmholtz had invented. In later years Bell said that had he read German fluently he might never have begun the research that led to the telephone.

Bell gave practically all financial interest in his telephone patents to his wife. He was not interested in business and preferred instead to pursue his research interests. His father-in-law, an attorney for a company that leased shoe-sewing machines, managed the patents. He established the principle that the telephone would be rented rather than sold.

In its early years, the Bell Telephone Company was run none too successfully by a conservative group of New England investors. After several reorganizations, AT&T emerged in 1900 as the parent company of a group of operating subsidiaries. Under the leadership of Theodore Vail, beginning in 1907, the company established the basic framework for the Bell System as it exists today.

Vail consolidated all research at one facility, the Western Electric plant in New York City. This was the forerunner of Bell Laboratories and the reason Vail has been called the originator of modern industrial research.

In a move uncharacteristic for businessmen of his day, Vail welcomed government regulation. He genuinely believed that the telephone industry was a "natural monopoly" and that the nation's best interests would be served by having just one privately owned but government-regulated telephone system. He foresaw chaos if the industry were allowed to fragment.

Financially, the system that Vail built proved to be exceptionally stable. AT&T gained its reputation as a "widow's and orphan's stock" during the Thirties when it maintained its dividend during the Great Depression. Most other corporations cut their dividends during this period.

Bell Laboratories, AT&T's research arm, has produced many of this country's most important technological advances, including television transmission, the transistor, the laser, the silicon solar cell, and the communication satellite.

In 1974, the government filed an antitrust suit in an effort to break AT&T up. The suit still continues. If fully litigated, the case will probably not be resolved until at least 1990. Paradoxically, should the government win, the result would probably be beneficial to AT&T shareholders. The reason is that the marketplace would probably place a higher total value on the pieces of AT&T (Western Electric, Bell Labs, the Long Lines Division, and the operating companies) than it does on the integrated company. This has been the typical market response when companies have been split up by decree in the past. The result of the dissolution of the Standard Oil Trust in 1911 provides an example of this phenomenon.

In a landmark decision, the FCC recently gave approval for "Ma Bell" to have a baby. Specifically, the FCC ruling allows AT&T to set up a subsidiary already dubbed "Baby Bell" which would be allowed to compete in information processing and other fields unhampered by government regulation. The FCC will continue to regulate AT&T's conventional phone system. Baby Bell will give AT&T tremendous growth opportunities. Its creation should prove very beneficial to AT&T stockholders in the long run. In the short term, however, it may temporarily retard earnings somewhat as there will be substantial expenditures involved in organizing the subsidiary.

Based upon the method outlined in Chapter 1 of Part II, we project that AT&T stock will rise in price from $54 to $122 a share by the end of the decade—an increase of 126 percent.

CHAPTER 31
INTERNATIONAL HARVESTER

ITHOUT CYRUS McCORMICK, the founder of International Harvester, the United States as we know it probably would not exist. The reason is that without the reaper, invented by McCormick, the North most probably would have lost the Civil War. The reaper freed tens of thousands of young men from harvesting and allowed them to do battle against the Confederacy. At the same time it kept up the supply of bread to the Union Army. As Lincoln's Secretary of War, Edward Stanton, stated, "Without the reaper, I fear the North could not win, and the Union would be dismembered."

Cyrus and his father first successfully demonstrated the reaper in Virginia in 1831. However, they did not immediately exploit the commercial potential of the invention. Instead, they went into the iron business. It was only after their iron business failed that they began manufacturing reapers. They shifted their business from Virginia to Chicago to be closer to the prime market for their machines.

By 1848, the patent on the reaper had expired. Cyrus attempted to get it extended only to be defeated in court by a competitor, who, ironically, was represented by Abraham Lincoln. The loss of the patent, however, did not thwart McCormick. His innovative business practices kept his company in a dominant market position.

McCormick's most important innovation was an early form of installment buying. A farmer could have a reaper for a small down payment with the rest due after the harvest. If the crop was poor or misfortune befell the farmer, McCormick gave him more time.

McCormick also realized that farmers were slow in making up their minds. Most would wait until their grain was almost ripe before ordering a reaper. To accommodate this tendency, McCormick set up nineteen assembly plants at strategic locations in the Mississippi river valley so that his machines could be assembled immediately and transported to nearby fields without delay.

In addition, McCormick understood that to remain successful his company must deliver a superior product to the customer. McCormick promoted field days, where rival reapers were tested on a ripe field of grain. Since his machines usually won, he received excellent local publicity. But more important, he was able to monitor his competition and stay abreast of new developments. He incorporated any worthwhile advances into his own reapers.

In 1902, the McCormick Harvesting Machine Company was merged with Deering Harvester Company to form the present International Harvester. In the early 1900s, the company developed high-wheeled vehicles for farmers. Out of this business, a substantial truck-manufacturing business developed.

In the Seventies, International Harvester ran into problems. It spread itself too thin. It was attempting to compete against Deere in farm machinery, Caterpillar in construction equipment, and General Motors in trucks. At the same time, it was developing a substantial turbine business. The result of attempting to spread its resources over such broad areas was that it did poorly in all. Against lesser competition it might have gotten away with reduced capital improvements and lower research and development budgets—but not against Deere, Caterpillar, and General Motors.

To rejuvenate the company, the directors brought in a Xerox executive, Archie McCardell. Under McCardell, International Harvester made impressive strides in cost-cutting. Unfortunately, his demand for work rule concessions from the UAW triggered a six-month strike in 1980, which resulted in heavy losses. Aftereffects of the strike, coupled with high interest rates and slow sales, have resulted in very serious financial problems for the company.

Currently the company is working on a $4.7 billion debt restructuring with its banks. The company has also been forced to sell off its profitable turbine division to raise cash.

Even if the company survives its present financial difficulties, we believe that its long-term viability will be severely damaged. The reason is that one of the requirements the company's bankers will surely insist upon is that available cash be employed to pay back their loans instead of being used for aggressive capital expenditures and product development. This will result in a further erosion of the company's long-term competitive position relative to Deere, Caterpillar, and General Motors, which are all moving forward rapidly.

We anticipate that at some point in the Eighties, International Harvester will be deleted from the Dow Jones Industrial Average. It will probably be replaced by either Caterpillar or Deere.

Since we don't believe that International Harvester will be in the Dow at the end of the decade, we have not projected a 1989 price for the stock. That is why no data appear at the start of this chapter.

CHAPTER 32
CONCLUSION

THIS BOOK HAS attempted to do something that Wall Street frequently fails to do—focus on the long term. Unfortunately, it is all too easy to become overwhelmed by short-term negative developments and lose sight of a very positive long-term outlook. As this book is being completed, investors are being buffeted by news of skyrocketing interest rates, increasing federal deficits, and a possible recession. It is understandable how investors can become very pessimistic in such an environment.

None of these developments, however, alters the fundamental forces that are driving corporate values dramatically upward. The Dow companies, in aggregate, will make billions of dollars in profits in 1982 and 1983 in spite of all the negative news. They will retain much of this money to invest in new assets. Their underlying values will further increase as inflation boosts the replacement cost of existing plant and equipment. Inflation will also continue to put more dollars in the hands of investors—dollars that at some point will find their way into the stock market under the influence of favorable capital gains tax rates. These are the fundamental realities—the realities that are being temporarily obscured by the current pessimism.

We fully expect this book to be greeted by skepticism. In fact, we will be disappointed if it isn't. Investors should be skeptical of new investment ideas. They should subject them to intense critical scrutiny. We are convinced, however, that as investors examine closely the logic and evidence we have presented, they will come to the realization that the stage is set for a dramatic rise in the American stock market in the 1980s.

We have attempted to be very specific in this book. We have made actual price forecasts for the Dow Jones Industrial Average and each of the thirty stocks that compose it. So that the reader can follow how our projections are working out, we will publish a summary sheet each year through 1989 showing the actual results compared to our projections for price, Return on Book Value, Payout Ratio, and Price/Earnings Ratio.

There will be no charge for this statistical summary. Data for each year will not be updated until May 1 of the following year. The data will be adjusted for stock splits. Otherwise a person several years from now might look up the price of Procter & Gamble and, finding it at $79, might conclude that our forecast for that stock was significantly in error. If Procter & Gamble had split three for one in the meantime, that $79 really would be the equivalent of $237 (3 × $79).

To receive this summary, send a stamped (first class postage), self-addressed No. 10 envelope (4⅛ × 9½ inches) to:

> Thomas Blamer
> c/o GB Associates Inc.
> P.O. Box 9957
> Minneapolis, MN 55440